"We say that the Easter Vigil is the very center of the year's liturgy but have we any idea why? Often it is reduced to being just a slightly longer Saturday vigil Mass. This book by Boselli is not a 'how-to' book for improving celebrations, but rather seeks out the depths of why this night is so important to us. Using the themes of fire, light, word, water, and table he explores what Passover—Resurrection means to us in a theological poetry. This is a book to savor and discover—and it will make us long for better actual celebrations."

—Thomas O'Loughlin, professor emeritus of historical theology, University of Nottingham

"Look, if the date and time of the next Easter Vigil in your parish is not already reserved on your personal calendar, there may not be much I can do for you. But read this book. It will reorient your calendar. And your life—if you're brave enough to change."

—Fr. Paul Turner, pastor of the Cathedral of the Immaculate Conception, Kansas City, Missouri, author of *Glory in the Cross: Holy Week in the Third Edition of* The Roman Missal

"Goffredo Boselli's *Fire of Love, Water of Life* celebrates the 'Mother of all Vigils' in a riot of paschal colors: the Christian mystery born in the darkness of fire, proclamation, water, and sacrament. With an excellent and very readable translation by Barry Hudock, the author unspools the centrality of the liturgical expression of faith in Christ's resurrection at the heart of this night of nights. After exploring this fine work, I could not help carrying the Christian community's exultant witness in my heart as an indelible sign of God's enduring love and covenant. This text serves as a superb inspiration for any Catholic Christian and will be of great practical use to pastors and catechists shepherding those in the Order of Christian Initiation of Adults."

—Guerric DeBona, OSB, professor of homiletics,
Saint Meinrad School of Theology

"This is a groundbreaking and contemporary commentary based on traditional sources from the Bible through to contemporary philosophers, theologians, and poets. It is to be savored, not read, and should be an extraordinarily valuable resource for catechumens, candidates, and sponsors, especially during Lent preceding their joining the Church at Easter."

—Kevin W. Irwin, dean emeritus, School of Theology and
Religious Studies, The Catholic University of
America, Washington, DC

Fire of Love, Water of Life

*Exploring the Meaning and
the Beauty of the Easter Vigil*

Goffredo Boselli

Translated by Barry Hudock

LITURGICAL PRESS
Collegeville, Minnesota

litpress.org

Originally published as *Domenica di Risurrezione: O notte beata!* by Goffredo Boselli

© 2023 Edizioni San Paolo s.r.l.
Piazza Soncino 5 – 20092 Cinisello Balsamo (Milano) – ITALIA
www.edizionisanpaolo.it

1   2   3   4   5   6   7   8   9

Library of Congress Cataloging-in-Publication Data

Names: Boselli, Goffredo, author. | Hudock, Barry, translator.
Title: Fire of love, water of life : exploring the meaning and the beauty of the Easter Vigil / Goffredo Boselli ; translated by Barry Hudock.
Other titles: Domenica di Risurrezione. English
Description: Collegeville, Minnesota : Liturgical Press, 2024. | "Originally published as Domenica di Risurrezione: O notte beata! by Goffredo Boselli, 2023 Edizioni San Paolo."—T.p. verso | Summary: "In Fire of Love, Water of Life, liturgical theologian Goffredo Boselli focuses upon Easter Vigil, the central moment of the church's year, helping readers understand how those who celebrate the Easter Vigil experience the very essence of Christianity. This book is a resource for presiders, homilists, liturgists, liturgical scholars, and all laity who want a more profound grasp of this most important celebration of the Christian year"— Provided by publisher.
Identifiers: LCCN 2023043392 (print) | LCCN 2023043393 (ebook) | ISBN 9798400801198 (trade paperback) | ISBN 9798400801204 (epub) | ISBN 9798400801280 (pdf)
Subjects: LCSH: Catholic Church. Liturgy and ritual. | Vigils (Liturgy) | Easter service. | BISAC: RELIGION / Christian Rituals & Practice / Worship & Liturgy | RELIGION / Christianity / Catholic
Classification: LCC BV176.3 .B6713 2024 (print) | LCC BV176.3 (ebook) | DDC 264—dc23/eng/20231127
LC record available at https://lccn.loc.gov/2023043392
LC ebook record available at https://lccn.loc.gov/2023043393

Contents

Introduction

EASTER: THE CENTER OF CHRISTIAN LIFE

"If Christ has not been raised, then empty is your faith" (cf. 1 Cor 15:14). These words of the apostle Paul are certainly among the clearest and most radical statements of the entire New Testament. It is a declaration that requires no explanation and allows for no debate. In the paschal mystery, we are faced not only with the most important truth of the Christian faith, but with its very foundation. Without the resurrection of Christ, the Christian faith is not simply deprived of something; it is emptied. There is nothing left—not like there is nothing left in an empty container, but like there is nothing left in a lifeless body. If there is no resurrection of Christ, there is no possibility of Christianity. It is no coincidence that in the profession of faith, before confessing "I believe in the resurrection of the dead," the believer says, "I believe in Jesus Christ . . . who rose from the dead on the third day." Christians believe that the dead will be resurrected *because* they believe Jesus rose from the dead and not the other way around.

Drawing out the implications of the apostle's statement, one could say, "Without the paschal mystery, your liturgy is empty." Indeed, if the resurrection of Christ is the foundation of faith, it is also, necessarily, the foundation of Christian liturgy, which is none other than the celebration of the paschal mystery. This is true in the case of every liturgy, but it is especially so for the annual feast of Easter. If the Sacred Triduum is the center of the liturgical year, the Easter Vigil is the heart of the Triduum. For this reason, the Easter Vigil is the church's most important liturgy; it celebrates the mystery of Christ's victory over death, which is the substance of every Christian liturgy.

The Easter Vigil, the church's longest and most elaborate liturgy, in which the most extensive arrangement of biblical readings is proclaimed, is the celebration that is richest in rites and symbols, most abundant in texts and songs, most intense in signs and gestures. For those who take part in it, it is the most demanding liturgy and, at times, probably also the most tiring. But it should also be the most engaging due to its beauty and the most intense due to the depth of its message. Those who celebrate it must be aware that in the Easter Vigil, they are experiencing the essence of Christianity and, at the same time, have in their hands the most intimate reality of the Christian message, because the resurrection of Christ is the heart of the Gospel. For this reason, the community as a whole must be accompanied in understanding the meaning and value of the fundamental signs, through a biblical-liturgical and spiritual introduction that allows them to enter the long celebration of the Vigil. Celebrating these rites wisely means not watching them passively but inhabiting them, recognizing them as both an expression and a nourishment of one's faith.

Presbyter and ministers

The role of the presbyter who presides over and guides the celebration is an important one. More than in any other liturgy, he must first internalize "the breadth and length and height and depth" (see Eph 3:18) of the mystery he celebrates. This is essentially an act of faith, not a performative capacity or ability, because the mind and the heart of the presbyter must be fully engaged in what he is called to say and do. Only if he has accomplished this progressive assimilation will his body, postures, gestures, and tone of voice be able to interpret and express the paschal faith that the church confesses through these ancient rites. This liturgy calls not for executors but interpreters.

The guidance and direction of a celebration are not wholly identified and even less exhausted by the one who presides over it; they extend also to the other ministers and the various ministries they carry out—above all the altar servers, lectors, and cantors who are at the service of the participation of the assembly. For those who carry out these roles, it is not enough to know what to do and what it means; they must have mastery of the dynamics of the entire celebration, the times to observe and the rhythm to mark. The quality of the community's participation and involvement in the celebration of the Vigil will depend to a great degree, if not completely, on how these ministers experience it firsthand.

The Easter Vigil: model of liturgy

More than any other celebration, the Easter Vigil demonstrates a Christian community's ability or, conversely, inability to celebrate with decorum and dignity. The complexity of the Holy Week rites is proof of this. If there is ordinarily, Sunday after Sunday and feast after feast, no care for the liturgy—that is, if there is scant attention to or preparation for the proclamation of the readings, the service of altar servers, the songs, the order and beauty of the liturgical space—it will not be possible for the same community suddenly to become capable of celebrating the Easter Triduum with dignity. One must arrive at it liturgically prepared, and this preparation is not simply the result of a concentrated effort at the time but the fruit of constant attention and habitual commitment to the celebrations that take place during the course of the year. The 1988 circular letter *Paschalis sollemnitatis*, on the preparation and celebration of the Easter feasts, recalls that the participation of the assembly in the Easter Vigil also depends on the quality with which the liturgical gestures and actions are performed: "The first part [of the Vigil] consists of symbolic acts and gestures, which require that they be performed in all their fullness and nobility so that their meaning, as explained by the introductory words of the celebrant and the liturgical prayers, may be truly understood by the faithful."[1]

A community capable of celebrating cannot be improvised; it is developed over time through education, patience, and attention. Carefully celebrating the rites of the Sacred Triduum and in particular the Easter Vigil does not mean doing extraordinary things, striving for dramatic effects, let alone extravagant ones; it means doing what the ritual requires with seriousness, simplicity, and beauty that is commensurate with the real capabilities of the community. If a community is too small and lacks the capacity to support a full celebration of the Vigil, it might join another community in mutual cooperation and support. In this way, a

1. Congregation for Divine Worship, Circular Letter *Paschalis sollemnitatis* (January 16, 1988), n. 82. (This document is not available on the Vatican website. See https://www.ewtn.com/catholicism/library /preparation-and-celebration-of-the-easter-feasts-2169. —Trans.)

parish's Easter Vigil can achieve in its truth and intensity the same beauty as the solemn liturgy of a cathedral.

This little book is not intended to be an introduction to the meaning of the Easter Vigil nor a pastoral aid or technical guide to the celebration. We will not consider the history of its development, nor will we comment on the individual parts in an exhaustive way. We will focus only on the major elements that characterize it and make it unique: it is a nocturnal Vigil during which the symbolism of fire, darkness, and light plays a decisive role in expressing the message that it conveys. The Liturgy of the Word articulates the essential stages of the history of salvation, from its beginning to the dawn of Easter, rereading it in the light of the proclamation: "Christ is risen!" The paschal candle is placed next to the ambo to signify that Christ's Passover illuminates the most important pages of the Holy Scriptures with new light.

Too often ignored is the fact that in this Vigil, Christ's passage from death to life is narrated through the primary elements of the life of human beings and of the world: light, water, word, bread and wine and, therefore, table. There is no biological life where there is no water and light, just as there is no authentic human life where the table of bread and word—that is, nourishment and relationship, the wine of celebration and joy—is missing. Yes, the mystery of life is celebrated through the holy mysteries that are the fundamental symbols of life.

The meaning of *mystery*

In the New Testament, the concept of *mystery* with regard to God does not refer, as in pagan mystery cults, to a mysterious reality, hidden and veiled from humanity, synonymous with an *enigma* or *puzzle*. The mystery of God, a mystery "kept secret for long ages" (Rom 16:25), was revealed by God in the life of his Son Jesus to the point of identifying it with him: "The mystery of God [is] Jesus Christ, and him crucified" (cf. 1 Cor 2:1-2), recalls the apostle Paul. God the Father has revealed all of himself, and in a definitive way, through Jesus Christ, making himself fully known not only to Israel but to all humanity. Christ is not simply the revealer of the mystery of God; he himself *is* the mystery of God. His whole life, culminating in his death and resurrection, is the highest summit of the revelation of the biblical God. The Passover of Jesus is the mystery of God. Every year in the celebration of Easter, the church confesses that the paschal mystery and the mystery of God are one and the same mystery.

If, according to the New Testament, only the mystery can fully reveal the mystery, we can also say that only the celebration of the paschal mystery fully reveals the paschal mystery. It reveals it more than any theology, any magisterial text, any catechesis, teaching, or preaching. Unlike theology, words alone are not enough for the liturgy to narrate and celebrate the richness of the life of Christ.

If, according to the ancient adage, the church believes as it celebrates, this means that the church *believes* the paschal mystery as it *celebrates* the paschal mystery. The quality of every believer's and every Christian community's faith in the risen Christ can be seen in the way they celebrate his resurrection.

Chapter 1

The Liturgy of Light

The cosmic Passover: where every living thing is reborn

The Easter Vigil begins outside the church. This is not only because there is a fire to be lit but also because Easter is the feast of the spring new moon, of creation coming back to life—for the Canaanites, the first inhabitants of Palestine; for the people of Israel; and finally for Christians, who have never forgotten this origin. The liturgy of the Vigil is, more than any other liturgy, a *cosmic* liturgy, because the celebration of Christ's resurrection is one with the rebirth of nature, which, when the frost and winter darkness is over, comes back to life with the onset of spring. For every creature and for every living being, Easter is the celebration of life that conquers every death, and spring is its great metaphor.

This, then, is why the Easter Vigil begins outside: so that believers may be aware of their communion with creation which is reborn to life. What is at stake here is the cosmic scope of Easter. The body of the Risen One is the matrix of a transfigured universe. And so before the paschal fire is lit, the assembly should be helped, with a few simple words, to grasp the cosmic dimension of Easter, inviting them to a time of silence for prolonged listening. The silence that opens the Vigil is not just any silence; it is the culmination point of the day of great silence, Holy Saturday, which at its end relinquishes its silence to the day of resurrection. It is the silence of pain for the death of Christ and in him of every innocent victim of human injustice, of stunned and mute suffering. But it is also the silence of waiting, the silence of love that stands vigil, the silence of hope. The silence that welcomes those who celebrate the Vigil is also the silence of the bells, of the organ, and of every musical instrument that, after the singing of the Gloria of the Lord's Supper on the evening of Holy Thursday, fell silent until the Gloria of the night of resurrection.

At that moment, those present at the Vigil find themselves not only in silence but also in the dark, and it is precisely when one can see nothing that the sense of hearing is most acute. Thus the first act of the celebration should be to listen to the night, recognizing its noises, its sounds, the song of animals, the rustling of trees, in the awareness that everything that lives has a voice. Easter is the celebration of the awakening of nature, which also brings with it the return of the voices and calls of creatures that the wise person knows how to recognize and the person of faith hears as moans that rise from the earth. In Christ every creature returns to life, and his victory over death is the principle of that promise made to every living being of "a new heaven and a new earth" (Rev 21:1), which one day will be fully fulfilled.

All creation celebrates this paschal night. Every being that has a breath of life celebrates its Easter, which is the passage from death to life. Thus in the short time of silence and listening that precedes the beginning of the Vigil, every believer gathered in the liturgical assembly feels that she is not only a creature among creatures, but a creature *with* creatures, realizing her vocation of being a priest of creation, the voice of every creature and interpreter of the desire for life, for liberation from mortality, and for salvation that she shares with every living thing. She makes her own what Paul describes as creation's own "eager expectation . . . in hope that creation itself would be set free from slavery to corruption and share in the glorious freedom of the children of God" (Rom 8:19-21).

In the heart of the night

The Easter Vigil begins outside the church in the darkness of night. Darkness, with the disorientation and discomfort it brings, is the first element of the strong impact of this celebration. The community that gathers is unable to easily see and recognize each other's faces. The darkness of the night and the absence of light is the concrete situation and the bodily experience that, without the need for words, becomes by itself the symbol of the spiritual and existential condition into which the announcement of Christ's victory over the darkness of death arrives. Darkness, however, not only envelops us; it dwells within us. Indeed, it is what we *were* before we shared in the light of the Risen One: "For you were once darkness, but now you are light in the Lord" (Eph 5:8).

The Vigil is celebrated at night, but the night is not simply one of its elements; it is rather an indispensable condition: without night, there is no Easter Vigil. "The entire celebration of the Easter Vigil must take place during the night, so that it begins after nightfall and ends before daybreak on the Sunday," reads the rubric of *The Roman Missal*.[1]

The onset of night, therefore, precedes the beginning of the Vigil; darkness must already have fallen when the community gathers to welcome it and to celebrate Easter in the entirety of its mystery and its truth. The Vigil can last as long as the night lasts; the night is the very matter of the Easter Vigil. Night is not simply the part of the day that falls between sunset and sunrise; it is much more than an astronomical reality. In human thought—of which philosophy, art, literature, and poetry are among the highest and most noble expressions—night is a metaphor for the state of those who live in ignorance, error, decadence, or barbarism. It is the obscuring of conscience and knowledge in the darkness of the unknown, of nothingness, of oblivion. The liturgy fully adopts these meanings of the night, which, moreover, are present throughout the Bible, from beginning to end. The liturgy turns the night from a metaphor into a symbol, that is, into a reality that expresses and at the same time communicates the paschal mystery. The liturgy therefore needs the night to celebrate the resurrection of Christ, because it is in darkness that light shines. For this reason, the night is part of the rite; it is the very matter of the Easter rites as much as are the fire, the candle, the flames, the baptismal water, the bread and the wine of the Eucharist.

1. *The Roman Missal*, 3rd edition (Collegeville, MN: Liturgical Press, 2012), 343.

"O truly blessed night" is the great song that resounds at the beginning of the Easter Vigil. Christians have always celebrated Easter in the night, because Christ rose from the dead not at sunset on "that solemn Sabbath day" (cf. John 19:31), not at dawn on the first day of the week, nor at noon when the light is at its peak. Rather, it was *in the night* that he rose from the darkness of the grave. It is in the night that life triumphed over death as a light that defeats the darkness, as a brightness that illuminates the darkness. The Risen One does not suppress the night but makes it the hour in which his life, and that of every creature, is restored.

Easter does not take away any of the nights that humanity has experienced through its millennia of history nor the nights that every human being can know: the night of war, when darkness blinds the minds of rulers and "darkness covers the earth, / and thick clouds, the peoples" (Isa 60:2); the night of senseless violence and gratuitous evil, of horrific injustice, of innocent pain and suffering that takes one's breath away; the night of love betrayed; the night of abandonment and loneliness; the night of depression and despair that are so well known to those who no longer have anything or anyone to hope for, a clouding of the spirit that often leads to the darkest night of those who take their own lives; and above all, the night of death, which remains, even after the dawn of Easter, the radical injustice, the extreme meaninglessness of life.

We Christians celebrate the resurrection of Christ in the heart of the night because the risen Christ did not eliminate the night, let alone spare it. The Risen One inhabits the night with us, shares it with us, having himself known the darkest darkness of the betrayal of his friend, of the abandonment of the disciples, and of the silence of the Father: "*Eli, Eli, lema sabachthani*"—"My God, my God, why have you forsaken me?" (Matt 27:46). This great night unites us. It makes us brothers and sisters, contemporaries of men and women of every time and place.

"O truly blessed night," the cantor repeats in the Easter Proclamation, the *Exsultet*, the song of the messenger announcing the paschal victory. It is a text that dates back to the fourth century—composed in the Po valley of northern Italy and, for this reason, traditionally attributed to Ambrose of Milan—and has never ceased to resound since then in the Easter vigils of the Western churches, albeit with variations and in different versions. This true song of the night repeats several times "*Haec nox est*"—"This is the night," recalling that the night of the Easter Vigil bears within itself every night of salvation:

> This is the night,
> when once you led our forebears, Israel's children,
> from slavery in Egypt. . . .
>
> This is the night
> that with a pillar of fire
> banished the darkness of sin.
>
> This is the night
> that even now, throughout the world,
> sets Christian believers apart from worldly vices
> and from the gloom of sin. . . .
>
> This is the night,
> when Christ broke the prison-bars of death
> and rose victorious from the underworld.

This proclamation is less a *laus cerei*—praise of the candle—than a *laus noctis*, praise of the night of Christ's resurrection, which it calls "truly blessed night" and God's "night of grace." The cantor, in the name of the whole assembly of believers, addresses the night directly, as if addressing a person who is present in that place and at that moment:

> O truly blessed night,
> worthy alone to know the time and hour
> when Christ rose from the underworld!

No one saw Christ rise again, and for this reason the text avoids saying that the night saw it. But it affirms that that night is the only one that knows *tempus et horam*. In a certain sense, the night of the resurrection is the first to celebrate the Risen One. There is not only the day and hour of Christ's resurrection; there is also the *time* of resurrection, which cannot be reduced to the moment and instant in which it occurred. It is not a measurable and quantifiable chronological time, *chrónos*. Rather, it is *kairós*, not simply a favorable time but a time that belongs to the resurrection. It is its *own time*, unique and yet running through the whole of history up to today. It is unrepeatable yet eternal time, not measurable chronologically but experienced by its essence and quality.

While theology rightly affirms that the resurrection of Christ is not a historical fact in the sense that it happened beyond history, the *lex orandi* reminds us in its own language that the resurrection has its own time and for this reason time belongs to it and it belongs to time. Though beyond history, the resurrection of Christ changed history and for this reason remains inscribed in the time of the world and in the history of humanity until the end. This is the reason that, in the liturgy of light, the numerals of the current year are engraved with a stylus on the paschal candle.

The *Exsultet* continues:

> This is the night
> of which it is written:
> The night shall be as bright as day,
> dazzling is the night for me,
> and full of gladness.

According to this Proclamation, of the night of Christ's resurrection "it is written"—that is, the Holy Scriptures speak of this night, the night narrated by Psalm 139:11-12, in which the psalmist describes his experience of the presence of the Lord as follows:

> If I say, "Surely darkness shall hide me,
>   and night shall be my light"—
> Darkness is not dark for you,
>   and night shines as the day.
>   Darkness and light are but one.

Like the great ancient liturgical texts, the *Exsultet*, too, obviously depends on the Greek version of the Hebrew Bible called the Septuagint, which renders Psalm 139 thus: "I said: Certainly the darkness will crush me, but the night will be illumination in my delight." The version provided by the Targum is significant: "Not even the darkness is dark for your word." In his commentary, the medieval French rabbi Rashi of Troyes renders the line, "Darkness and light are but one" as "to you they are both the same." By making the images of the psalm its own through the singing of the *Exsultet*, the liturgy reminds the believer that in his life of faith he can go beyond the human distinctions between darkness and light, because the resurrection of Christ allows him to know them and to live in another way. The night does not disappear, does not become day. It is not day but *nox sicut dies*; it remains night, but a night that shines "as bright as day," to the point of being "dazzling."

The night of the Easter Vigil is marked by the polarity of darkness and light, a metaphor for the fundamental human polarity of death and life. They are radical opposites that the Easter liturgy does not try to hide or smooth out but that maintain a constant tension between one another, through oxymorons such as singing of the luminous night. The night is a source of light and is an experience of illuminated darkness, just as death is conquered by the Risen One but human beings continue to die believing in life stronger than death. It is at the heart of the mystery of death that Christ is continually in the act of resurrection, so that death at the very heart of glory gives the measure of the depth of the paschal mystery. These are reflections of the paradox of paschal faith. Only those who live die, and those who believe that death has been overcome are mortal beings. If it is true, as the Orthodox Easter troparion sings, that Jesus "with his death tramples on death," it is equally true that it was his whole life and not just his way of death that defeated death. In the way he lived his mortal life, Jesus opened the way for humanity to a life-giving death.

The *Exsultet* continues in its song of the night:

> The sanctifying power of this night
> dispels wickedness, washes faults away,
> restores innocence to the fallen, and joy to
>   mourners. . . .
>
> O truly blessed night,
> when things of heaven are wed to those of earth . . .

The first reality that rises with Christ is therefore the night itself, which is transformed from a biblical metaphor of evil, guilt, and sin until it coincides with the resurrection of Christ, to the point that the proclamation uses the expression "[t]he sanctifying power of this night" as a synonym of resurrection. Easter night and the resurrection of Christ are one. The night, from a mysterious reality of darkness, becomes a mystery of light and salvation; it becomes the nocturnal matrix of the Christian faith, a fertile womb of new children of light reborn to new life.

THE NEW FIRE

The Easter Vigil opens with the lighting of a fire, as if to say that the resurrection of Christ is not a rite to be performed but a fire to be lit. Fire is a primordial natural element, a powerful reality, an inexhaustible symbol of life and passion. The Victorian poet Leigh Hunt referred to "the most tangible of all mysteries—fire."

But fire is, above all, a vital *reality* for humanity, one of the most important assets that humanity alone has been able to ignite, control, and protect for nearly half a million years. Thanks to this ability, fire has brought radical changes to human life—from defending oneself from the dark and cold, to cooking food, to inhabiting space. Fire has made a decisive contribution to humanizing life, giving humanity a significant advantage over animals.

In myths and many ancient religions, fire is one of the highest manifestations of the divine. Suffice it to recall the myth of Prometheus, in which the Titan, deceiving Zeus who had hidden fire from humanity, steals it from Olympus to bring it to earth. The importance of Prometheus's act is found in the fact that in Greek mythology, fire is a symbol of divine strength and the power of knowledge given by the gods to humanity so that it may grow and progress.

In the biblical story of the Exodus, it is from the fire of a bush that burns without being consumed that God entrusts Moses with the mission of freeing the children of Israel from Egypt. From the very fire of the burning bush, God reveals for the first time his name, "I AM" (see Exod 3:1-15). And in the theophany that seals the covenant, the Lord descends in fire: "Mount Sinai was completely enveloped in smoke, because the LORD had come down upon it in fire" (Exod 19:18). In the Bible, fire defines God's identity and represents the power of both his anger and his love, his passion and his jealousy for Israel: "The LORD, your God, is a consuming fire, a jealous God" (Deut 4:24). The prophet Jeremiah describes God's seductive power as an overwhelming fire that burns within him:

> [I]t is as if fire is burning in my heart,
>   imprisoned in my bones;
> I grow weary holding back,
>   I cannot! (Jer 20:9)

Later it will be God himself who reminds the prophet of his experience: "Is not my word like fire?" (Jer 23:29). And how can we forget that fire is also an element of divine judgment, a biblical image taken up in the responsory *Libera me* in the Office of the Dead, with the expression "*Dum veneris iudicare saeculum per ignem*"—"when you shall come to judge the world by fire."

In the gospels, John the Baptist announces that one mightier than he "will baptize you with the holy Spirit and fire" (Luke 3:16), so that the baptism of Jesus is an immersion in fire, a symbol of the Holy Spirit, a flame of purification, testing, refinement, and transformation. Even the psalmist, aware of his own innocence, prayed (in words that might be translated literally): "Examine me, Lord, and test me; / burn my reins and my heart" (Ps 26:2). Reflecting upon a similar translation, Augustine of Hippo comments: "How are you going to burn my affections? With the fire of your Word. And how will you burn my heart? With the heat of your Spirit, of which scripture says elsewhere, *No one can hide from his heat* (Ps 18:7[19:6]). And of this same fire the Lord says, *I have come to set fire to the earth* (Luke 12:49)."[2]

Augustine recalls that Jesus described himself as one who came to set the earth on fire, expressing a desire or perhaps a dream: "How I wish it were already blazing!" (Luke 12:49). How can we forget the similar *ágraphon*— that is, words of Jesus not found in the canonical gospels but quoted, in this case, by both Origen and Didymus the

---

2. Augustine of Hippo, "Exposition 2 of Psalm 25," n. 7, in *Expositions of the Psalms, 1–32*, trans. Maria Boulding, OSB, The Works of Saint Augustine, III/15 (Hyde Park, NY: New City Press, 2000).

Blind and present in the Gnostic Gospel of Thomas: "Whoever is near me is near fire."[3]

And so the community gathered around the fire at the beginning of the Easter Vigil has before it not only an archetypal symbol of humanity but also the intense and evocative reality that Jesus used to describe himself as a person devoured by interior fire, expressing the great passion that was the origin of his words and actions throughout his life. His task on earth was to sow the seed of fire that is the word of God, a fire that burns in the heart of every living being—"How I wish it were already blazing!" With his death on the cross and his resurrection, Jesus lit that fire that he'd come to bring with his person, which is none other than his Gospel. The fire of the Vigil is the fire of the Gospel, and Christ's Passover is a fire for the world—not to burn the world, but to make it burn with love!

The Easter fire therefore becomes a symbol of the rabbi of Nazareth and of his passion for humanity. Enzo Bianchi summarizes this in his commentary on Jesus' words about fire in Luke 12:49:

> Jesus is a man of great and deep desire, a man of passion, and here he suddenly confesses this passion that inhabits him. That the fire of the Spirit that he brought from the Father to earth, a fire of love, should set the world on fire and burn in the heart of every human being—this he strongly desired!

3. *The Gospel of Thomas*, trans. Stephen Patterson and Marvin Meyer, The Gnostic Society Library, http://gnosis.org/naghamm/gosthom .html, n. 82.

He wanted it in the days of his earthly life, and he still wants it today, because the fire he brought is often covered by ashes that the church itself puts on it, preventing it from burning. Yes, we know it's true: one only has to read the entire history of the Christian faith to realize that the fire of the Gospel flares up here and there, from time to time, in people and communities who stir up its embers, but then soon, too soon, it is covered up again with ash. It provides some warmth, it is kept alive and preserved, but it certainly doesn't burn. . . . Jesus wanted it to burn in the hearts of believers as it burned in the hearts of the two disciples on the road to Emmaus, when the Scriptures explained by the Risen One caught fire; he wanted it to burn as it burned in the church born of Pentecost.[4]

How can we forget Abraham Heschel's observation that "religion is born of fire, of a flame, in which the dross of the mind and soul is melted away,"[5] but then it runs the risk of living on the outskirts of the fire. Refusing to keep to the margins of that fire from which our faith originates, we Christians, on the vigil of our most important feast, begin by lighting a fire and gathering around it, thus expressing that the Gospel of Christ is the center of our community and of the lives of us who have met and known the one who came "to set the earth on fire" (Luke 12:49).

4. "Fuoco, immersione, divisione," https://www.monasterodibose.it /fondatore/riflessioni-sul-vangelo/10718-fuoco-immersione-divisione/.
5. Abraham Joshua Heschel, *God in Search of Man: A Philosophy of Judaism* (New York: Farrar, Straus and Giroux, 1955, 1983), 317.

The great fire that opens the Easter Vigil is, then, the symbol of passionate and therefore jealous love, a noble and demanding sentiment that the Lord nourishes for his people and that reaches its fullness in the story of Jesus' love unto death. It embodies "the flame of Yah," the burning love of which the Song of Songs speaks:

> For Love is strong as Death,
> longing is fierce as Sheol.
> Its arrows are arrows of fire,
> flames of the divine. (Song 8:6)

The fire of the Easter Vigil inflames with passion and love for the Lord the whole liturgy of this holy night, and it is, at the same time, the image in which every believer who celebrates Christ's resurrection sees his own heart reflected. It is a heart that, like those of the disciples of Emmaus, burns as it hears the word of the Risen One opening all the Scriptures that speak of him. As the Italian poet Mario Luzi wrote in his *Libro di Ipazia* (Book of Hypatia): "It is in fire that one must burn; nothing suits the word more than the temperature of fire."[6]

The symbol of fire characterizes the Easter journey, which began with the ritual of placing ashes on the head at the beginning of Lent. In the natural course of things, fire leads to ashes, but in the Easter journey, on the contrary, the reminder of the human being's condition of dust leads to his vocation to be a participant in the flames of the Lord's love. Each person is ash destined to become fire—this is the transformation that the resurrection of

6. Mario Luzi, *Libro di Ipazia* (Milan: Rizzoli, 1980), 85.

Christ brings about. From the ashes placed on the head as a sign of the path of conversion, believers arrive at Pentecost to receive the "tongues as of fire" (Acts 2:3) of the Holy Spirit on their heads.

From the ashes, the Easter journey leads believers not to a generic fire but to the "new fire," as the liturgy's Blessing of the Fire describes it:

> O God, who through your Son
> bestowed upon the faithful the fire of your glory,
> sanctify this new fire, we pray,
> and grant that,
> by these paschal celebrations,
> we may be so inflamed with heavenly desires,
> that with minds made pure
> we may attain festivities of unending splendor.[7]

At the beginning of the celebration of Christ's Passover, there is a *new fire*—that is, a desire that, in order to be authentic "heavenly desires," must above all be a desire for the newness and rebirth of the human and earthly life of every believer as well as of the whole church. Fire, as we have seen, is an image of passion, so that the new fire of Easter is for Christianity a reminder of its evangelical vocation to be not only new wine that breaks old wineskins but also a new fire that burns with the passion and audacity of newness, first of all against the agony of oneself, the agony that Emmanuel Mounier described in 1946 and that today stands clearly before us: "When Christianity errs, let it at least err in grandeur, in audacity, in defiance, in adventure, in passion. But Christianity be-

---

7. *The Roman Missal*, 344.

coming confused with social shyness, with a balancing act and blind fear—that we can never allow."[8]

The flame of the paschal candle is lit by the new fire of each year in which the feast of Easter is celebrated. The numbers of the solar year are inscribed with a stylus on the candle itself, telling us that that Easter cannot be experienced by the church as one of the many Easters, like the Easter of the previous year and even less as an Easter out of time, but as new life capable of renewing the Christianity that—infused with the grandeur, audacity, adventure, and passion of the Gospel—lives in the *today* of the world.

The Easter Vigil is the only liturgy that calls for burning a fire, one that, because of the symbolic value we have briefly recalled here, is not only functional to the lighting of the paschal candle but has an indisputable relevance in the rite that requires authenticity and beauty. The circular letter *Paschalis sollemnitatis* instructs: "Insofar as possible, a suitable place should be prepared outside the church for the blessing of the new fire, whose flames should be such that they genuinely dispel the darkness and light up the night."[9]

The church asks, then, that this fire, as a liturgical sign, be a real fire produced by the combustion of wood, and not of artificial material, a fire that is started and grows until it flares up, illuminating the dark and creating a fascinating environment for the celebration. Such is the primordial value and the symbolic impact of fire that it

8. Emmanuel Mounier, *Agonia del cristianesimo?* (Vicenza: La Locusta, 1960), 33.

9. *Paschalis sollemnitatis*, n. 82

must be prepared and made with care to arouse the enchantment of those present. The fire of the Easter Vigil must be as beautiful and arresting as the reality it symbolizes. When a liturgical sign is paltry, when it is badly made and patched together, its meaning is diminished, its value is nullified, and its effect is minimized. Therefore easy substitutes, such as embers, are to be avoided. So are functional but reductive choices that might technically be called fire but lack strength and effectiveness. This is why *Paschalis sollemnitatis* n. 82 expressly recalls the truth of fire as a sign. Indeed, opening the most solemn liturgy of the church with a fire so meager that it is incapable of lighting up the night fatally compromises the opening of the celebration and inevitably marks all that follows.

Before gathering around the table of the Word, which is the ambo, and around the source of new life, which is the baptismal font, and before sitting down at the table of the Body and Blood of Christ, which is the altar, the community gathers around the fire that warms hearts as much as bodies, illuminates faces, and creates a bond. It is the charcoal fire that the Risen One approached on the shore of the lake to prepare a meal for the disciples, inviting them to come and eat (see John 21:12). That, too, was a paschal fire; indeed, it is the first paschal fire, which has never been extinguished since that day and that Christians hand down from generation to generation on Easter night.

The flame of a candle

In a famous essay called *The Flame of a Candle*, the poet and philosopher of science Gaston Bachelard has written:

Long ago, in a long ago even dreams themselves have forgotten, the flame of a candle made wise men think; it provided the solitary philosopher with a thousand dreams. On his table, next to the objects imprisoned in their shapes, next to those books that teach one so slowly, the flame of the candle summoned endless thoughts and aroused immeasurable images. For a dreamer of worlds at that time, the flame was among the world's phenomena. The system of the world was studied in large books, and now a simple flame—oh mockery of erudition!—insists upon its own enigma. Is not the world alive in a flame? Does it not have a life of its own? Is it not the visible sign of some innermost being, the sign of some secret power? Does it not hold within itself all the internal contradictions that make an elementary metaphysics dynamic? Why search the dialectics of ideas when the dialectics of fact and being exist at the heart of a single phenomenon? The flame is a being without substance, but for all that it is strong. . . .

In the presence of a flame, we communicate morally with the world. Even in a simple vigil the flame of a candle is the model of a tranquil and delicate life. The slightest breath will certainly disturb it, just as an alien thought will disrupt the meditation of a meditating philosopher. But when the reign of full solitude truly arrives, when the hour of tranquility truly sounds, then the same peace resides in the heart of the dreamer as in the heart of the flame and then the flame preserves its form and rises directly, like a resolute thought, towards its vertical destiny. . . .

But for the wise man that I imagine, the lesson of the flame is greater than the lesson of falling

sand. The flame calls the vigilkeeper to raise his eyes
from his folio to quit his working time, his reading,
his thinking time. Within the flame, even time
holds its vigil.

Yes, he who keeps a vigil before the flame no
longer reads. He thinks of life. He thinks of death.
The flame is precarious and courageous. The light
is destroyed by a breath, relit with a spark, easy birth
and easy death. . . .

A candle extinguished is a sun that dies. The
candle dies even more gently than a star in the sky.
The wick bends; the wick blackens. The flame has
swallowed its opium from the shadow that em-
braces it. And the flame dies a good death; it dies
in its sleep.[10]

From the new blessed fire is taken the flame with which
the paschal candle is lit at the words: "May the light of
Christ rising in glory / dispel the darkness of our hearts
and minds." And then the deacon, raising the candle, sings
out, "The Light of Christ." And the community replies,
"Thanks be to God."[11] This is repeated three times, each
time the deacon raising the candle higher and raising his
tone of voice until "The Light of Christ" becomes a song
and the assembly's "Thanks be to God" a cry of joy, a song
of blessing, a sound of victory. This is an intense and highly
symbolic moment. The cry "The Light of Christ" pierces
the silence just as the flame of the paschal candle pierces
the darkness. The flame of a candle raised in the dark of

---

10. Gaston Bachelard, *The Flame of a Candle*, trans. Joni Caldwell
(Dallas: The Dallas Institute, 1988), 13, 14, 16, 17.
11. *The Roman Missal*, 346.

night is the symbol of Christ the light of the world, and here is depicted the essence of the Christian faith and its paradox: the light of Christ who rises again and scatters the darkness in the heart of the world is like the faint, unobtrusive light of a candle flame. The symbol of the flame of the paschal candle raised and acclaimed three times announces that the light of Christ is not a splendor that dazzles, not a truth that blinds and overpowers; it does not have the dull force of self-imposing evidence but the meekness of a flame of light and heat that, due to its fragility, must be kept and protected.

But the flame of the paschal candle is not the only flame, unique and unrepeatable, because all who are present then light the candles they hold from that flame, and the light of the paschal candle extends little by little, meaning that every believer receives the light of Christ, carries it in her hands, and guards it. On the day of baptism, each newly baptized is given a candle that is lit from the paschal candle. We are born into the faith with a candle flame in hand. And later, at our funeral, the paschal candle placed next to our coffin is a reminder of that flame from which the flame of our faith was born and to which it returns in death.

The progressive diffusion of light, as the candle of each person in the assembly is lit, is one of the most evocative and moving moments of the Easter Vigil. No one produces that light on his own; we can only receive it from the flame of the paschal candle. Receiving the flame and in turn transmitting it to those nearby is an intense gesture that expresses the reciprocal giving of light, a sign that faith in the risen Christ is received as a gift that one does not keep jealously for oneself, but in turn gives it, and by giving it, it is transmitted. The light that is offered from one believer to another creates a communion, so that the light that is spread is the light of communion. Ecclesial communion has its own light, and it is the light of the Easter Vigil.

The first effect of the candle flame held in each hand is the illumination of each person's face and nothing more, reminding us that every believer has her own recognizable face, which attests to her uniqueness, personality, experience, and original and unrepeatable history. Being reborn with Christ to new life means understanding that no longer being prisoners of death and hell coincides with recognizing the faces of others as the faces of brothers and sisters, according to the words of the evangelist: "We know that we have passed from death to life because we love our brothers. Whoever does not love remains in death" (1 John 3:14).

The light of the new Easter fire illuminating so many faces reveals a profound truth that is often missed, namely that before any technical description and erudite definition, the church is a community of faces—faces that look at each other and recognize each other as the faces of brothers and sisters to be loved: "Whoever loves his brother remains in the light" (1 John 2:10).

We should acknowledge that in the current Roman rite, the first part of the Easter Vigil, the Lucernarium, risks being not very festive and failing to express Easter joy. In light of this, songs and acclamations could accompany the different gestures. For example, the slow propagation of light among the assembly could be accompanied by the song of light that has come down to us, the *Phos*

Hilaron, the ancient christological hymn that dates from the late third or early fourth century:

Phos Hilaron (Song of Light)

R. O radiant light
eternal splendor of Father
the holy and blessed Jesus Christ.

Gathered in the midst of night
contemplating the new light,
we sing to the Father and to the Son
and to the Holy Spirit of God. *R.*

You are worthy to be praised
by holy voices of every time,
Son of God who gives life,
the universe proclaims your glory. *R.*

Behold the night that shines brighter than day
the night that glows brighter than the sun
the night that burns brighter than fire
the night that proclaims the Passover. *R.*

O Christ, you have destroyed death,
you have triumphed over the enemy,
you have trampled the underworld and emptied it,
you have raised humanity to the heights of heaven. *R.*

You are the Alpha and the Omega,
the unutterable Beginning and End,
you sit now at the right hand of the Father
but you will come to transfigure the earth. *R.*[12]

12. Monastery of Bose, *La Pasqua del Signore: Liturgia del cammino pasquale* (Magnano: Qiqajon, 2011), 91–92.

Easter celebrates the light that is the experience of life. To be born, to become part of the world, is precisely to come to light. Together with water and air, light is the natural element that creates the conditions for life to emerge and to grow, and for this reason it is synonymous with birth and life. Since ancient times, the symbolism of light has captivated and accompanied human thought. Light allows us to see, to understand, to distinguish, in a constant dialectic with the darkness that is its opposite, the enemy to be defeated. Philosophy, science, religion, wisdom, which make it the symbol of knowledge, beauty, and harmony, have always been nourished by the experience of light: the blinding brightness of the sun, the flashes of a fire, the delicate light of a candle flame. Light has always been one of the metaphors most loved by artists. For poets it is the substance of images. For architects it is the creator of spaces and forms, to the point that "architecture is the skillful, rigorous, and magnificent play of volumes brought together in light" (Le Corbusier).

According to the biblical story of creation, "*jehî'ôr*"— "Let there be light" (Gen 1:3)—is the first word pronounced by God while "the earth was without form or shape, with darkness over the abyss" (Gen 1:2). Before any source of light—before the sun, the moon, or the stars— God's word *jehî'ôr* brings about the light that cannot be seen but makes one see. The gift of light is God's will of love and life for creatures. For this reason, every living being, the plant as well as the human being, seeks, desires, and naturally goes towards the light and not towards darkness, because light is life and darkness is death. John opens the Fourth Gospel with the hymn that proclaims the Word as the true light, and further on he identifies Jesus himself with the light: "I am the light of the world" (John 8:12). Among the New Testament authors, John is the master of light. He manages to synthesize the entire revelation of Jesus in the light itself: "Now this is the message that we have heard from him and proclaim to you: God is light, and in him there is no darkness at all" (1 John 1:5).

In the Easter Vigil, light is more than a symbol; it is a sacramental matter that accomplishes what it signifies. The "light of the risen Christ" cannot be reproduced but is proclaimed, depicted, represented, evoked in the light of the Easter Vigil that shines in the many flames of the fire, which is all gathered in the single flame of the paschal candle and then spreads again in many small flames, generating a light that envelops everything and everyone in a "kindly light." With the light of a fire becoming the flame of a candle, the Vigil begins as a celebration of light, in the knowledge that there is not enough darkness in the human heart nor in the entire world to extinguish the light of a single candle.

We walk in the light

If darkness inspires fear and forces immobility, light sets us on the road and opens paths. Even in the Easter Vigil, the first effect of the light is to set believers in motion, to make them a people on the move. Those gathered around the fire then set off towards the interior of the church, and the light of the flame of the paschal candle guides them, directs them, encourages them. The community of believers walking in the dark is the memorial of the people of Israel who on the night of liberation were guided by the pillar of fire: "The Lord preceded them, in the daytime by means of a column of cloud to show them the way, and at night by means of a column of fire to give them light. Thus they could travel both day and night" (Exod 13:21).

If the pillar of cloud is the image of the glory of the Lord, the pillar of fire is the flame of the Lord's love that consumes. The book of Numbers sees in the pillar of fire the manifestation of the presence of God who is in the midst of his people and, at the same time, walks before them, guiding them like a shepherd: "You, LORD, are in the midst of this people; you, LORD, who directly revealed yourself! Your cloud stands over them, and you go before them by day in a column of cloud and by night in a column of fire" (Num 14:14).

The Easter Proclamation, the *Exsultet*, expressly identifies the paschal candle with the pillar of fire, thus offering a significant example of liturgical exegesis of the Scriptures according to the logic of anticipation that is proper to typology. The cantor, speaking on behalf of the celebrating community, says:

> [N]ow we know the praises of this pillar,
> which glowing fire ignites for God's honor,
> a fire into many flames divided,
> yet never dimmed by sharing of its light,
> for it is fed by melting wax,
> drawn out by mother bees
> to build a torch so precious.[13]

In addition to considering the Exodus's pillar of fire a prophecy of the paschal candle, these lines make reference

---

13. *The Roman Missal*, 356.

to the entire rite of the Lucernarium, which concludes with the singing of the *Exsultet*—its beginning with the new fire and its splitting into the many flames of the candles of those present that does not, nevertheless, extinguish its splendor. It should be noted that this passage of the Easter Proclamation is the only instance in which a liturgical text makes explicit reference to the very rite in progress; in the act of celebration, the assembly itself becomes a mystagogy of the rite it is celebrating and the mysteries it contains.

The procession into the church is not only a reminder of the liberation journey of the children of Israel; it is also a symbol of the journey of believers of all times. The believer is a person who walks in the dark holding nothing but the flame of a candle, a figure of her faith, as if to say that only those who have been able to walk the paths of the night reach dawn. Jesus Christ said of himself and of his disciples: "I am the light of the world. Whoever follows me will not walk in darkness, but will have the light of life" (John 8:12). Yes, faith in Christ illuminates and warms the little that is enough, and that the believer must accept as enough, on the journey of life. Sunlight allows one to see everything clearly and precisely; the light of a candle flame or a lamp, on the contrary, illuminates just enough to take a few steps forward. Like someone who walks in the night with only a candle's flame for light, the believer through her faith cannot claim to have clarity on everything and to understand the meaning of everything; she is prevented from living by unshakeable truths, by absolute certainties. "We walk by faith, not by sight" (2 Cor 5:7), the apostle Paul reminds us, and thus the believer understands by experience rather than by intellect the meaning of the psalmist's words: "Your word is a lamp for my feet, / a light for my path" (Ps 119:105).

The flame of a candle is not a stable and immobile reality; by its nature, it constantly flickers. Even this flickering is an image of faith, of faith's restlessness and of its being alive and vibrant, its being a reality that is exciting and captivating but also oscillating and trembling. The restlessness of faith is above all a restlessness for the Gospel, as Pope Francis recalled in a tweet in 2018: "Holy restlessness for the Gospel is the only restlessness that gives peace."[14] It is also the restlessness and fatigue of a faith that, not content with being a mere "Sunday component of life," knows the inexhaustible search for truth, as Ernesto Balducci has recalled with his usual lucidity: "For some, religion is only a Sunday component of life, a formal respect for family traditions, a convenient pretext for not feeling the restlessness and fatigue of the personal search for truth, as if faith constituted a kind of guarantee, on the basis to which man can be considered exempt from the duty of sweating for his own spiritual bread."[15]

Like the light of a flickering flame, faith, too, is constantly threatened: a single gust of wind, even a gentle one, can put it out. "The light is destroyed by a breath, relit with a spark," Bachelard wrote in his essay. The procession on the night of the Vigil reminds the believer that he is not alone, that in his life of faith he walks together

14. Pope Francis (@Pontifex_it), Twitter, October 1, 2018, https://twitter.com/Pontifex_it/status/1046723906709598208.

15. "'Maggio di cultura Cristiana,' oggi incontro sul pensiero di Ernesto Balducci," ManfredoniaNews.it, May 12, 2014, https://www.manfredonianews.it/2014/05/12/maggio-di-cultura-cristiana-oggi-incontro-sul-pensiero-di-ernesto-balducci/.

with other men and women who hold candles in their hands, forming with them a community that is always ready to rekindle his flame, which is the light of his faith, the luminosity of the meaning of his life, the flame of his love and his desire to hope. Albert Schweitzer wrote: "Sometimes our light goes out, but it is rekindled by another human being. Each of us should thank from the bottom of our hearts those who rekindle that light." Who hasn't experienced at the Easter Vigil the flame of his candle being blown out by the spring breeze? When that happens, whoever is next to us rekindles our candle with the light of their own flame. This, too, is one of the most poetic images of what it means to be part of the community of people who share the light of faith in Christ's resurrection, which is the light of the new commandment: "If we walk in the light as he is in the light, then we have fellowship with one another" (1 John 1:7). Certainly, it is more useful to keep the flame burning in the dark than not to feed the fire.

The church is the community of women and men of faith whose purpose is not to enlighten itself or even just to enlighten one another; the community of believers in Christ, rather, shares the condition of all people, that of being immersed in darkness. Like everyone else, Christians, too, do not know what tomorrow will bring, and in the dark they try to find a way to be lights, to shed light despite the darkness, to enlighten those in need.

As we mentioned above, this first part of the Easter Vigil often takes place in a rather subdued atmosphere that expresses little Easter joy, since the rite does not include acclamations or songs—although the letter *Paschalis sollemnitatis* states: "To each response, Thanks be to God, there is no reason why there should not be added some acclamation in honor of Christ."[16] In fact, the ritual cannot and in some ways must not provide for everything; rather, the concrete context may inspire creativity. The procession to the church must not resemble a funeral procession; it should resemble a joyful dance of believing men and women who, holding the flame, go towards the house of the community to experience the Lord's Passover. The cantor might sing the paschal troparion of the Orthodox tradition. Set to music in a simple and appealing form, it may be repeated several times as a refrain by the congregation:

> Christ is risen from the dead,
> trampling down death by death,
> and upon those in the tombs bestowing life!

Kindly light

As the faithful enter the church with lit candles, the darkness of its interior is gradually dispelled. The slow expansion of the light throughout the liturgical space is not like the instantaneous turning on of the electric lights to which we are accustomed; it is the growing diffusion of a tenuous light, the coming to light of an almost unreal evocative light. What happens at the Easter Vigil evokes not only a theology of light but a true poetics of the light of liturgical space that all the modern electrical lighting of our churches should take as an inspiring model and criteria of authenticity. There is therefore no reason that,

16. *Paschalis sollemnitatis*, n. 83.

once in the church, the candles held by the assembly must now be extinguished as their light is overcome by the turning on of the church's electric lights.

The *ars celebrandi*, on the contrary, suggests that the special light created by the innumerable flames of the candles is the most suitable light for listening to the Easter Proclamation and the readings from the Old and New Testaments. It evokes the image of a sage, bent over the sacred page, scrutinizing the holy Scriptures by the flame of a candle. The church's electric lights could be turned on, accompanied by the sound of the organ and bells, as the assembly begins to sing the Gloria; this was the custom at the Easter Vigil in Paris's Basilica of Notre Dame (until the fire of 2018) and continues to be in the city's church of Saint Sulpice.[17]

This experience of light is unique to this circumstance; it is distinctive and unrepeatable. Thus the light of the Vigil is capable of creating a liturgical setting that is intimate, discreet, spiritual, almost familiar. The experience certainly evokes the light to which John Henry Newman referred—indeed, to which he prayed—on June 16, 1833, in the bay of Capri, as "kindly light."

The ancient chant of the Easter Proclamation, both a hymn to the night and a hymn to light, resounds in the surreal light created by the sum of the slender light of the candles of all the faithful. Each worshipper's hand becomes a candlestick, a reflection and truth of the great candlestick on which the paschal candle now stands, above everything and everyone, and from whose flame

---

17. See "Vigile Pascale a Notre-Dame de Paris," KTO TV, https://www.youtube.com/watch?v=2D7zj5IoX7I.

each of their smaller candles was lit. The light of the flame of the paschal candle alone could not illuminate the entire church, making the faces of the assembled brothers and sisters recognizable and distinguishing their bodies, but together with the many flames of these believers, the light increases and extends, reaching everything and everyone. It is, so to speak, a synodal light: there is not one that illuminates everyone, but each brings his own contribution of light.

This unique and suggestive light creates the perfect environment for the proclamation of the *Exsultet*. That is to say, it makes it possible, since it allows the cantor to sing of the night brighter than the day.

THE EASTER PROCLAMATION

When the whole community is in the church, the deacon, priest, or cantor intones the Easter Proclamation, the *Exsultet*. We have already commented on this text in its main parts. Some communities, in Italy and elsewhere, alternate the Easter Proclamation with the singing or reading of a text attributed to John Chrysostom, *Eis tòn hághion Páscha*, thus alternating with the Latin *Exsultet* a possible Eastern form of the same message.[18] Other communities use adaptations of the *Exsultet*; below we offer two significant examples of sound and respectful revisions of the liturgical text that may allow for their greater under-

---

18. For an Italian adaptation of the text of Pseudo-Chrysostom, see Monastery of Bose, *La Pasqua del Signore*, 95–96; and for a shortened form, André Gouzes, *La notte luminosa: Iniziazione al mistero della Pasqua* (Magnano: Qiqajon, 2015), 134–35.

standing by the assembly and include further biblical and existential enrichment.

The first is taken from the Easter liturgy of the Monastery of Bose. Taking the traditional text as a foundation, it brings the Easter Proclamation back to its biblical roots, focusing on the four memorable nights of humanity that we will discuss later. Most of the text is entrusted to a cantor, while the assembly intervenes by singing short festive acclamations:

> Let the multitude of angels rejoice in heaven,
> Rejoice, servants of the Lord,
> let the shofar resound a song of glory,
> for the Lord has risen from the dead.
>
> *R. Christ is risen, hallelujah!*
>
> Let the earth rejoice, flooded with great splendor:
> the light of the King of the ages
> has conquered the darkness of the world.
>
> *R. Christ is risen, hallelujah!*
>
> Let our mother church rejoice,
> shining with the glory of her Bridegroom,
> and this whole assembly resound
> with the acclamations of festive believers.
>
> *R. Christ is risen, hallelujah!*
>
> The Lord be with you.
> —And with your spirit.
> Lift up your hearts.
> —We lift them up to the Lord.
> Let us give thanks to the Lord our God.
> —It is right and just.

It is truly right and just
to express the exultation of the heart in song,
to give thanks, moved by the Spirit,
to the invisible God our Father
through Jesus Christ our Lord.

R. Christ is risen, hallelujah!

This is the night that the Lord
manifested himself to create the world:
the word of the Lord was light, and the light
     shone in the darkness,
and the darkness did not overcome it.

R. Christ is risen, hallelujah!

This is the night that the Lord
manifested himself to Abraham:
Isaac, his beloved son, was offered as a sacrifice,
Abraham received him back as risen
and this offering became a prophecy of resurrection.

R. Christ is risen, hallelujah!

This is the night that the Lord manifested himself
     to the Egyptians,
the blood of the Passover Lamb
was a sign of salvation for Israel,
our fathers were freed from slavery
and passed unharmed through the Red Sea.

R. Christ is risen, hallelujah!

This is the night that Jesus the Messiah rose from
     the dead:
the chains of death were broken,
hell was emptied forever
the sin of the world was forgiven.

R. Christ is risen, hallelujah!

O blessed night, brighter than day,
O night of the wedding of the Lamb,
you announce the coming eternal Easter,
you are the sign of the glorious manifestation of
    the Lord!

R. Christ is risen, hallelujah!

The second example of an adaptation of the *Exsultet* is a text written by Don Michele Do (1918–2005), a charismatic Italian priest who established at St. Jacques in the Aosta Valley a community of fraternal welcome and wise celebrations. Compared to the previous one, this adaptation offers a more existential and anthropological interpretation:

May the creatures of the heavens and the creatures
    of the earth rejoice,
because the mystery of existence
has found clarity this night.
May the earth, penetrated by such light, rejoice,
having laid aside all its darkness.

May the Church be the space where the
    expectations of all peoples
find their fulfillment and are expressed in song.
Therefore, dear brothers and sisters,
grateful for such a clear light,
together we sing of God's mercy.

It is truly right and just
that all the passion of the heart and mind
give praise to the invisible God
the Almighty Father and to his only-begotten
    Son Jesus Christ,
who has shown us new heavens and new earth.

This is the night that frees the slaves of every Egypt,
the night in which all the Red Seas are crossed to
    find freedom.
This is the night that illuminates with its light
the dark depths of every person.

This is the night that brings together all believers
    in Christ,
spread throughout the earth
  and, freeing them from their burdens,
restores them to beauty, grace, and holiness.

This is the night when Christ,
   in the captivity of death,
rises victorious from all the hells of humanity.
It would be worthless to be born if life did not
    have a meaning
    and a divine fullness.

This is the night where even sin is grace.
O truly blessed night
  whose time and sacred hour only you have known
when Christ rose from the depths of death
  and abandonment!
This is the night that fulfills
  humanity's eternal yearning
and of which is written: "And the night will be
  clear as day."

The miracle of this holy night dissolves the
    darkness,
purifies the heart, restores innocence
to those overwhelmed by evil,
dispels hatred, creates communion,
and breaks the arrogance of every power.

O truly blessed night, in which earthly things
    unite with heavenly ones
and divine things join human ones!
In the grace of this night, welcome, O Father,
our offering symbolized by the Easter candle.

We therefore pray to you, Lord,
    that the light of this candle,
lit to dispel our gloom,
    may never fail
and rise to you welcome as a star among your stars.

Let its light unite and mingle
    with the light of the Morning Star,
the star that knows no sunset:
your Christ who, having reemerged from the
        underworld,
shines serenely on humanity's path.[19]

19. Don Michele Do, *La gioia della fede di Pasqua: l'Exultet.*

Chapter 2

The Liturgy of the Word

The mother of every Liturgy of the Word

The Easter Vigil's Liturgy of the Word is the mother of every Liturgy of the Word. Indeed, on Easter night, the assembled church has the paschal experience of hearing the fundamental biblical texts of the history of salvation in the light of Christ's resurrection. The paschal candle is placed next to the ambo, not for functional or aesthetic reasons but to signify that the pages of the Old Testament are heard, meditated upon, interpreted, and prayed in the light of the flame of the paschal candle that illuminates them; the light of the Risen One reveals their meaning and allows their understanding. Easter night is a luminous night because it is illuminated by the light that the pages of the Old and New Testaments radiate.

St. Jerome wrote that "ignorance of the Scriptures is ignorance of Christ," and this truth is always valid in the life of the church and of every believer. But the annual celebration of Easter, and in a very special way the Easter Vigil with its program of biblical readings, is the precise moment in which Jerome's axiom is revealed in all its truthfulness. The believer and the Christian community who ignore the Scriptures proclaimed in the Vigil ignore the risen Christ.

The path along which the Vigil's Liturgy of the Word guides the gathered Christian community is in all respects identical to the path of the disciples of Emmaus. On closer inspection, the journey upon which the Risen One takes them is not so much the geographical distance that separates Jerusalem from Emmaus but the spiritual distance between their image of Christ and that of Jesus, an image contained in the Scriptures that he himself will reveal to them: "Then beginning with Moses and all the prophets, he interpreted to them what referred to him in all the scriptures" (Luke 24:27). The path of the two disciples and that of the paschal liturgical community are an open path through the mystery of the Scriptures, a path that has as its guide the Risen One, who becomes the hermeneutic of what refers to him. In the following episode of Luke's gospel, Jesus comes into the midst of his community in Jerusalem and once again opens the disciples' minds to understand the Scriptures. If, on the journey to Emmaus, he referred to the law and the prophets, here he is even more exhaustive: "Everything written about me in the law of Moses and in the prophets and psalms must be fulfilled" (Luke 24:44).

Through the law, the prophets, and the psalms, Christ is his own exegete, and this is the spark that, at that time as today, ignites faith in his resurrection among the disciples, just as a spark ignites the new Easter fire. Thus in the Easter Vigil, the pages of Genesis, Exodus, the prophets, and the psalms are symbolically "all the scriptures," because they are, as we shall see, the fundamental pages both for Israel's faith in God the liberator and for the church's faith in Christ the Savior. Due to their relevance, those pages contain the meaning of "all the scriptures," so that the understanding of the biblical texts of the Easter Vigil is the apex and the source of the knowledge of the mystery of Christ that the church confesses. In the same way that the account of the crossing of the Red Sea by the people of God is the source of all the Scriptures of the Old Testament, so the Gospel of Jesus' resurrection is the origin of the New Testament.

Jesus' Passover is *secundum Scripturas*, as the church proclaims in its Creed: "He rose again on the third day in accordance with the Scriptures." This is to say not only and not so much that the Scriptures announced it but that in his life, as in his passion and death, Jesus obeyed the "it is written," because he read in it "it is written of me": "[It] is written of me in the scroll" (Heb 10:7; quoting Ps 40:7-9 LXX). The Targum thus renders this verse of Psalm 40 in Aramaic: "Then I said: I will enter eternal life if I have meditated upon what was written for me in the scroll of the book of the law." From "it is written" to "it is written *of* me" to "it is written *for* me." This is the understanding of the Scriptures of Jesus of Nazareth, the same understanding of the Scriptures to which the Spirit of the Risen One brings believers in him.

In shaping the various sets of readings to be proclaimed at the Easter Vigil over the centuries, choosing certain readings and not others, the church has affirmed that faith in the Risen One was born and still is born today from the pages of Scripture that are listened to on the luminous night of Easter. Faith in the resurrection of Christ is rooted in the understanding of those stories taken from the law of

Moses, the revelations of those prophets, and the praying of those psalms; and the Spirit of the Risen One opens the minds of believers of every generation to the knowledge of the mystery of Christ contained in the Scriptures, just as he, on Easter day, opened the minds of the disciples.

In the Vigil, the Christian community not only revives its own Easter faith but is itself the creator of that faith, confirming and strengthening it. It is a faith that that community received from the generations of believers who preceded it, but which it makes its own and renews above all in the Vigil in order to be able, in turn, to pass it on to future generations. The liturgical assembly of the Easter Vigil is the quintessential figure of mother church, and the Liturgy of the Word is her fertile womb from which she generates sons and daughters to faith in the risen Christ. This Liturgy of the Word is already, therefore, a baptismal font in which to be reborn to new life, because without the word of God, even the sacrament of baptism can do nothing; it is an ineffective and sterile rite.

The *Hebraica veritas* of the Christian Passover

Among the nine biblical readings of the Easter Vigil—seven from the Old Testament, a reading from St. Paul, and the gospel of the resurrection—the first three taken from the Pentateuch are, as we have already observed, the foundational texts of Israel's identity: the story of the creation of the world (Gen 1:1–2:2), the binding of Isaac (Exod 22:1-18), and the passage of the people of Israel through the Red Sea (Exod 14:15–15:1). These are followed by four readings taken from the prophets—two from Deutero-Isaiah, one from Baruch, and one from Ezekiel; providing the bridge from the Jewish Passover to the Christian Passover, these readings lead to the fourth night described in the Targums' "The Poem of the Four Nights," the messianic night, which, in the Christian perspective, is the night of the resurrection of Jesus and, at the same time, the night of the Messiah coming in glory: "At midnight, there was a cry, 'Behold, the bridegroom! Come out to meet him!'" (Matt 25:6).

The church cannot celebrate the Passover of Jesus Christ without listening to these biblical readings as a community, since the Christian Passover forms a whole with the Jewish Passover: Israel's liberation from slavery in Egypt is its birth as the people of God in the same way that Christ's Passover is the birth of the church. This is the reason for the church's insistence that the account of the crossing of the Red Sea must always be read at the Easter Vigil, even when pastoral circumstances suggest reducing the number of readings: "Never . . . should the reading of chapter 14 of Exodus with its canticle be omitted."[1] The Easter Vigil's cycle of biblical readings is among the most significant attestations of the unique history of salvation shared by Israel and the church, of the covenant that has never been revoked, and of the continuity of faith between the Jewish and Christian traditions.

In the wake of Roger Le Déaut and his work *La nuit pascale* (The paschal night),[2] for the past few decades an

---

1. *The Roman Missal*, 364.
2. Roger Le Déaut, *La nuit pascale: Essai sur la signification de la Pâque juive à partir du Targum d'Exode XII, 42* (Rome: Pontifical Biblical Institute, 1980).

increasing number of scholars have acknowledged the correspondence between "The Poem of the Four Nights" and the lectionaries of the Christian Easter Vigil, seeing in this link a convincing interpretative key of the choice of the proposed biblical readings. The heart of this "poem" —appearing in the Palestinian Targum whose texts are dated between the fourth and eighth centuries CE—is the night when the Lord freed Israel from slavery in Egypt, the night of *Pesah*.

Following the passage of Exodus 12:42—"This was a night of vigil for the LORD, when he brought them out of the land of Egypt; so on this night all Israelites must keep a vigil for the LORD throughout their generations"—the Targum comments:

> Truly, four nights are those that are written in the Book of Memorials.
>
> The first night: when the Lord was revealed over the world to create it. The world was without form and void, and darkness was spread over the face of the abyss, and the Memra of the Lord was the Light, and it shone; and he called it the First Night.
>
> The second night: when the Lord was revealed to Abram, a man of a hundred years, and Sarah his wife, who was a woman of ninety years, to fulfill what the Scripture says: Will Abram, a man of a hundred years, beget, and will his wife Sarah, a woman of ninety years, bear? And Isaac was thirty-seven years when he was offered upon the altar. The heavens were bowed down and descended, and Isaac saw their perfections, and his eyes were dimmed because of their perfections, and he called it the Second Night.

The third night: when the Lord was revealed against the Egyptians at midnight; his hand slew the first-born of the Egyptians, and his right hand protected the first-born of Israel to fulfill what the Scripture says: Israel is my first-born son. And he called it the Third Night.

The fourth night: when the world reaches its appointed time to be redeemed: the iron yokes shall be broken and the generations of wickedness shall be blotted out, and Moses will go up from the midst of the desert <and the king Messiah from the midst of Rome.> One will lead at the head of the flock, and the other will lead at the head of the flock, and his Memra will lead between the two of them, and I and they will proceed together. This is the night of the Passover to the name of the Lord: it is a night reserved and set aside for the redemption of all Israel, throughout their generations.[3]

The passage from the book of Exodus with which "The Poem of the Four Nights" opens and concludes inspires the Palestinian Targum to the point of presenting, as Mauro Perani rightly observes, "a rich interpretation of the night of Passover narrated in this verse. It expands its meaning, and the result is a new text, which becomes an interpretative key to the identity and history of Israel."[4]

Le Déaut pointed out that the third night, that of *Pesah*, is the heart of "The Poem of the Four Nights," as

3. *Targum Neofiti 1: Exodus and Targum Pseudo-Jonathan: Exodus*, trans. Martin McNamara, MSC, and Michael Maher, MSC, The Aramaic Bible, vol. 2 (Collegeville, MN: Liturgical Press, 1994), 51–53.

4. Mauro Perani, "Il Poema delle quattro notti nella rilettura del Targûm di Es 12,42," in *Parola spirito e vita* 79 (2019): 101.

it is the liberation of Israel from Egypt. "It is the founding act that constitutes the supporting wall of all Judaism, which not by chance will be conceived as a perennial actualization of that founding event of the Jewish religion. Nor can be forgotten the reverberation that that event will project upon Christianity through the person of Jesus of Nazareth."[5]

For this reason, this "mother night" is preceded in the poem by two other nights, the night of creation and the night of the calling of Abraham and the binding of Isaac, and it is followed by the messianic night, the night of the final eschatological fulfillment. These are the world's four crucial nights, and at the Easter Vigil the church celebrates Christ's resurrection by commemorating these four nights in which the Lord watched over his people, performing works of salvation for them.

The biblical readings provided by the Christian lectionaries for the Vigil dating back to the fifth century report the same biblical episodes evoked by the poem. Even today in the Easter Vigil of the Roman liturgy, as well as in other Christian liturgies, the first three texts provided correspond to the first three nights of the poem: the readings of the creation story, the binding of Isaac, and the crossing of the Red Sea. The subsequent readings of the Roman Lectionary, taken from the prophets Deutero-Isaiah, Baruch, and Ezekiel, correspond to the fourth night of the poem, the messianic night. Thus the lectionary of the Easter Vigil is one of the most important and eloquent attestations of the words of the apostle: "the root is holy" (Rom 11:16) which sustains the church; "consider that you do

5. Perani, "Il Poema delle quattro notti," 103.

not support the root; the root supports you" (Rom 11:18). Even the great biblical narratives that the church proclaims and listens to on Easter night—the story of creation, the binding of Isaac, and the crossing of the Red Sea—belong to the *radix sancta*. Because of its origins, the Christian faith has an intrinsic, permanent, and unique relationship with the Jewish people.

There is no better synthesis of this presentation of this interpretative key of the Easter Vigil's Liturgy of the Word—the key of the *Hebraica veritas*, to use the expression coined by St. Jerome—than what the biblical scholar Jean-Pierre Sonnet wrote with his usual lucidity in an important book on the readings of the Easter Vigil with the significant title *La Bibbia si apre a Pasqua* (The Bible is opened at Easter):

> At the moment of celebrating its own mystery, founded on the risen Christ, the church associates itself with the mystery of its other self, the chosen people. Gathering the foundational texts of the identity of the Israel of God—in particular, Genesis 22 and Exodus 14—in the context of the Easter Triduum means prolonging the Good Friday prayer for the Jews: "Let us pray for the Jewish people, to whom the Lord our God spoke first, that he may grant them to advance in love of his name and in faithfulness to his covenant." It will always be a paradox: the church cannot celebrate its own mystery without commemorating the mystery of Israel. Such is the mystery of the God of the promises.[6]

6. J.-P. Sonnet, "Le letture della Genesi: La creazione (Gen 1,1-2,2) e la legatura di Isacco (Gen 22,1-18)," in Sonnet, ed., *La Bibbia si apre*

IN THE LITURGY THE BIBLE REACHES ITS PASCHAL TRUTH

The second interpretive key to the Easter Vigil lectionary is found in understanding the liturgy as the living context of the Scriptures. On this luminous night, the biblical readings and the liturgical signs interact, illuminating each other with meaning in a true hermeneutical circle. A singular form of intertextuality is created not only between the various readings but also through correlations and references of meaning between the readings and the other rites of this liturgy—in particular those of the liturgy of light and the rite of baptism—each with its respective contents, symbols, and metaphors. In this way, in the Easter Vigil the Bible attains its original paschal truth.

Proclaimed, heard, and interpreted within the liturgy, the Holy Scriptures live in their natural habitat. Generated as the word of God within the womb of the liturgical assembly, the Scriptures find in it their most adequate living environment. They are there, according to the effective image of Louis-Marie Chauvet, "like a fish in water": "The Bible is in the liturgy like a fish in water. It is *constitutively* made to be proclaimed in the assembly (*qehal JHWH, ekklesía*) and not to be read at table and individually (without detracting anything from the legitimacy and fruitfulness of the latter practice). . . . The Bible never reaches its truth as it does when it is pro-

---

a Pasqua: Il Lezionario della Veglia pasquale: storia, esegesi, liturgia (Cinisello Balsamo: San Paolo, 2016), 65–81, here 67. This volume inspired and guided me in drafting the brief presentation of the Easter Vigil Lectionary. I refer to it for those wishing to deepen the topic.

claimed in the *ekklesia*, where the liturgy unfolds its constituent dimensions. One can therefore speak of a 'sacramentality' of the Scriptures, one that is not purely accidental but essential."[7]

If the faith of the confessing community generated the Scriptures, it is the faith of the community in prayer and listening that causes them to be continually reborn as a living word. Yes, without the Bible, the liturgy is nothing; it is like a body without a soul. And in turn, the Bible without the liturgy lacks its best part. Immersed and drawn into the dynamics of ritual, the Bible gives the best of itself. Certainly a story from the Pentateuch, an announcement from the prophets, or a biblical psalm have an undoubted objective meaning in themselves, as historical-critical exegesis demonstrates. However, the liturgical context in which they are read and heard—be it a feast day, a season of the liturgical year, or the celebration of a sacrament—illuminates them with new and different meanings, "other" meanings. This is not true in the sense of attributing additional contents to it, almost forcing the "it is written," but by drawing from the text all its inexhaustible riches of meaning ordered to the knowledge of the mystery of Christ and its actualization in the today of the believing community. In the Pontifical Biblical Commission's document on "The Interpretation of the Bible in the Church," we read: "The liturgy, and especially the sacramental liturgy, the high point of which is the eucharistic celebration, brings about the most perfect actualization of the biblical texts, for the liturgy places the proclamation in the midst

---

7. Louis-Marie Chauvet, *L'umanità dei sacramenti* (Magnano: Qiqajon, 2010), 40.

of the community of believers, gathered around Christ so as to draw near to God."[8]

Unique of its kind, the Easter Vigil's Liturgy of the Word is made up of three elements: readings, psalm responses, and prayers. The biblical text is first proclaimed, then prayed through the psalm, and finally completed in a prayer that provides an explicit Christian and paschal interpretation. The prayer, offering a Christian reading of the Old Testament passage that it follows, expresses with particular clarity the paschal faith of the church born from listening to the reading in the light of Christ's resurrection. Here more than ever, the liturgy expresses the words of the apostle: "Faith comes from what is heard" (Rom 10:17).

Through the admonition that introduces the Liturgy of the Word, the presider invites the assembly to assume the spiritual attitude typical of someone preparing for *lectio divina*. First of all, there is an invitation to listen: "[L]et us listen with quiet hearts to the Word of God." Then there is an invitation to meditation: "Let us meditate on how God in times past saved his people and in these, the last days, has sent us his Son as our Redeemer." And finally, there is an invitation to prayer: "Let us pray that our God may complete this paschal work of salvation by the fullness of redemption."[9] The liturgy itself—a *hapax* of all the liturgical books—understands listening to the word of God at the Easter Vigil as a true and proper *lectio*

---

8. Pontifical Biblical Commission, "The Interpretation of the Bible in the Church" (1993), available in English at https://www.bc.edu/content/dam/files/research_sites/cjl/texts/cjrelations/resources/documents/catholic/pbcinterpretation.htm.

9. *The Roman Missal*, 364.

liturgica composed of the three traditional steps: listening, meditation, and prayer. The first moment, the *lectio* proper, here becomes *obscultatio*, since in the liturgy the Scriptures are not read but heard.

From a properly theological point of view, the admonition specifies that the assembly is called to *listen* to the word of God contained in the pages of the Scriptures proclaimed; to *meditate* on the saving actions performed by God for his people in the old covenant and the redemption of the same people accomplished "in these, the last days" by the Son sent by him; and finally, to *pray* for the eschatological fulfillment of the salvation accomplished at Easter. Referring to "this paschal work" without being specific, this admonition holds the Jewish and Christian Passover together in a single Passover and, at the same time, looks to the eschatological Passover. In the *lex orandi* of the Easter Vigil, the church confesses that the Passover announced in the liberation of salvation of the people of Israel, fulfilled in the redemptive resurrection of Jesus, still awaits its final fulfillment in the eternal Passover, the eternal Easter. Through this admonition, the presider recalls that Easter is not an event that belongs only to the past and lies behind the assembly celebrating it here and now; rather, Easter takes place in the present and stands before the assembly as a reality that must be awaited and invoked. The fulfillment of Passover is in fact the object of prayer. In fact, we will see how the trinomial of *salvation, redemption, and fulfillment* characterize the interpretation of the Scriptures by those prayers that mark the Vigil's Liturgy of the Word.

The Bible teaches us to celebrate Easter

Few liturgical assemblies are adequately prepared to listen to and understand the entire succession of nine readings envisaged by the lectionary of the Vigil. Such listening and understanding would require a certain assiduity with the Scriptures, a familiarity with the fundamental elements of biblical culture, and training in listening, all of which goes beyond the capabilities of an ordinary liturgical assembly but might be possessed by a religious community or gathering of an ecclesial movement. The rubrics require the reading from Exodus 14, the one from Romans 6, and the gospel of the resurrection. Between the maximalism of the nine readings and the minimum threshold of the three indispensable ones, the ideal biblical path should include the story of creation, the binding of Isaac, and the crossing of the Red Sea as fundamental texts of Jewish identity, followed by one of the four proposed texts of prophecy, the reading from Paul, and the gospel.

The Lamb slaughtered from the creation of the world

During the Vigil, listening to the story of creation from the first chapter of Genesis leads the assembly to the creative act that marks the beginning of the history of salvation, which, if one looks closely, is also a passover: the transition from primordial chaos to life in all the forms and expressions of living beings, plants and animals, life that reaches its apex in the creation of man and woman. The incipit of the story of creation narratively immerses the assembly into the depth of the darkness that "[i]n the beginning" covered the abyss. It is in darkness that God's effective word resounds for the first time: "'Let there be light,' and there was light." Genesis narrates the experience that the assembly of the faithful listening to that story has just experienced at the beginning of the Vigil. A correlation is evoked between the first day of the week and the first act of the Easter Vigil: a night illuminated by light. There is no other occasion when the liturgy becomes the Bible-in-act as it does in this moment.

A second correspondence—perhaps less immediate, but certainly equally eloquent—is the creation of the human person by God: "God created [humankind] in his image." At the moment the lector reads, "God said: 'Let us make [human beings] in our image, after our likeness,'" all those present should feel called to attention and challenged, somehow called back into existence. They ought to be saying to themselves, "This is talking about me," and responding inwardly with a "Here I am!" It is almost as if the creation of humanity happens again in that moment and each one present is born into life. Accustomed to religious language, we easily forget that the Greek noun *anastásis*, which is usually translated as "resurrection," literally means "to rise from the dead" and in the divine passive "to be raised from the dead." On this night in which Christians celebrate the life of the Risen One who defeated death by being "raised from the dead" (Rom 6:9), upon hearing the story of the creation of humanity, believers might stand to demonstrate with their bodies that, as human beings, they are creatures of God and, as Christians, they are "raised with Christ" (Col 3:1). In raising Jesus from the tomb, God created the new Adam.

The responsorial psalm follows the reading. The Lectionary proposes two. The first, Psalm 104, is a contemplation of the power of God revealed in his creation:

> How manifold are your works, O Lord!
>> In wisdom you have wrought them all—
>> the earth is full of your creatures. (v. 24)

The second, Psalm 33, is certainly the best prayerful commentary on the creation story: "By the word of the Lord the heavens were made; / by the breath of his mouth all their host" (v. 6). This psalm is a joyful song that invites believers to sing to the Lord because with his word he acts faithfully and with his love he fills the earth. "The earth is full of the goodness of the Lord"—repeating this antiphon in song, the assembly confesses that creation is brimming with God's love.

As Ludwig Monti points out, "In these luminous words that, mixing cosmological and historical motifs, unite creation and redemption shines the insistence on the powerful word of God, mediator of his saving action: for God, to say is to do."[10] Prayed by the Christian community celebrating Christ's Passover, this psalm discloses a clear and natural christological interpretation of the word with which God created all things, which, moreover, the New Testament already explicitly confesses:

> All things came to be through him,
>> and without him nothing came to be.
> What came to be through him was life,
>> and this life was the light of the human race.
> (John 1:3-4)

10. Ludwig Monti, *I Salmi: preghiera e vita: Commento al salterio* (Magnano: Qiqajon, 2018), 400.

Following the reading and the psalm, the prayer concludes this first ritual section. The assembly stands, and in its name the presider prays:

> Almighty ever-living God,
> who are wonderful in the ordering of all your works,
> may those you have redeemed understand
> that there exists nothing more marvelous
> than the world's creation in the beginning
> except that, at the end of the ages,
> Christ our Passover has been sacrificed.[11]

This prayer articulates one simple plea: that Christians be enlightened to understand that Christ's Passover is a greater work of God than the very creation of the world. If in creation God manifested his love for humanity and for every living being, in the fullness of time "God so loved the world that he gave his only Son" (John 3:16), who in obedience took the form of a servant to the point of becoming "like a lamb led to slaughter" (Isa 53:7), "the Lamb slain," a crude image that means nothing other than that Christ is the Lamb who gave his life. The prayer explicitly refers to the figure of the Lamb and ends by quoting directly from St. Paul: "*Pascha nostrum immolatus est Christus*"—"our paschal lamb, Christ, has been sacrificed" (1 Cor 5:7). In both rabbinic literature and in Paul, Passover is synonymous with the Lamb. The link between the creation of the world and the sacrifice of the paschal Lamb evoked by the prayer evokes the apocalyptic image of the Lamb, slain "from the foundation of the world" (see Rev 13:8).

11. *The Roman Missal*, 365.

The Lamb is slaughtered not only *from* the creation of the world but also *because of* the creation of the world. The Lamb gave its life at the very moment in which God created the world out of love. In God, creating and giving life unto death coincide. That creation narrated by the reading of Genesis bears in itself the need for the Creator to suffer and to be put to death by his own creatures. The origin of the world bears, inscribed in itself, the mystery of innocent suffering. God's act of gratuitous love assumes from the beginning the form of the immolated Lamb, because free and liberating love contemplates from its birth the possibility of radical contradiction. Since the origins of the world, God's unconditional love has exposed itself, without any defense, to gratuitous evil, to radical injustice, even to the death of the innocent. The immolated Lamb is the price that the Father, the Son, and the Spirit are ready to pay for a freed creation, a liberated humanity.

This is the superiority of redemption over creation, because in Christ's Passover the truth of creation is fully revealed; it is the truth of the heart of the Father, the God of Jesus Christ. Only the innocent suffering of the Son brings reconciliation between the Creator and his creation.

Night of vigil for the Lord

The second sequence of the Easter Vigil's Liturgy of the Word that we will reflect on here is that of chapters 14 and 15 of the book of Exodus, divided into the reading of the story of the passage of Israel through the Red Sea (Exod 14:15–15:1) and the song of victory (Exod 15:16-18), also called the Song of Moses or the Song of the Sea. These two parts form a single, celebratory whole. At the end of the reading, in fact, the reader does not acclaim "the Word of the Lord" and the assembly does not respond "Thanks be to God"; rather, the last verse of the reading—"Then Moses and the Israelites sang this song to the LORD" (Exod 15:1)—provides the transition to the Song of the Sea. Thus the biblical text becomes the ritual action: the lector leaves the floor to the singing assembly. The prayer follows, and the Amen of the assembly concludes the section.

Like light, water belongs to the Easter symbolism both in the biblical readings of the Vigil and in the liturgical rites, but in the text of Exodus 14 it becomes a central element. In the account of creation, the first word of God is *light*, while the first action that God performs in the history of the world is to separate the waters, those above the firmament from those below it—that is, the waters in the heavens from those that form the seas. In Exodus 14, God commands Moses: "[L]ift up your staff and stretch out your hand over the sea, and split it in two, that the Israelites may pass through the sea on dry land. . . . Then Moses stretched out his hand over the sea; and the LORD drove back the sea with a strong east wind all night long and turned the sea into dry ground. The waters were split" (vv. 16 and 21). Moses, in obedience to God's command, stretches out his hand over the sea, but it is God himself who carries out the saving action: he is, in fact, the subject of the two verbs, *drove back* and *turned dry*, that result in the separation of the waters. "[T]he Israelites entered into the midst of the sea on dry land" (v. 22). The result obtained with the separation of the waters is identical to that described in the creation story, the emergence of dry land: "God called the dry land 'earth'" (Gen 1:10).

The appearance of dry land in the middle of the Red Sea, as in the middle of the waters under the sky in the creation story, attests to a new act of God the creator. In Genesis it is the work of God the Creator, while in Exodus it is the work of God the Liberator, to say that God creates the world and frees his people with the same gesture: separating the waters to bring out the dry earth on which his creatures may live. This action with which God *created* the earth is still the action with which God *creates* his people—creating a passage for them and therefore a *passover* from slavery to freedom. The dry land on which Israel walks is a prophecy of the promised land in which Israel will live a new life as a people saved by the Lord: "Thus the Lord saved Israel on that day from the power of Egypt. When Israel saw the Egyptians lying dead on the seashore and saw the great power that the Lord had shown against Egypt, the people feared the Lord. They believed in the Lord and in Moses his servant" (Exod 14:30-31).

In this last part of the reading, Israel is the subject of only two verbs: *saw* and *believed*. They are—certainly not by chance—the same verbs that the evangelist John attributes to the beloved disciple inside the empty tomb on the day of the resurrection: "He saw and believed" (John 20:8). Israel not only sees the dead bodies of the Egyptians but also sees the hand of the Lord, a seeing that, going beyond the obvious, penetrates reality. It is a seeing that is understanding and knowledge, a seeing that leads to faith. On the seashore the children of Israel confess the Lord as their God and recognize in the passage through the sea on dry land the origin of their history as God's people.

Seeing and believing move Israel to sing to the Lord. Here we are faced with the classic biblical sequence: the

Lord carries out the work of salvation, the people see and recognize the event as the work of the Lord and confess their faith in him, and, finally, they celebrate the Lord with song and feast. This is the structure that occurs regularly in both the Old and New Testaments: work of salvation, confession of faith, celebration in song.

The Song of Moses, a sort of *Te Deum* of Israel, celebrates the heart of the Jewish faith: "I will sing to the Lord, for he is gloriously triumphant; / horse and chariot he has cast into the sea" (Exod 15:1). As if a single person, Israel sings in the first person to the Lord, confessing who he is and what he did on that night for his people. Such is the intensity of the song that Israel comes to identify it with the Lord himself, "The Lord is . . . my song" (Exod 15:2, RSV), together with expressions that are clear confessions of faith: "This is my God, I praise him" (Exod 15:2). As a true model of the song of Israel, this text demonstrates that singing to the Lord means meditating on his works and narrating his wonders to proclaim his salvation. The Song of Moses is not only a memorial of the passage through the sea and the victory over the Egyptian army; it is also a prophecy of Israel's entry into the promised land and of the Lord's dwelling on the mount of Jerusalem where he will dwell in the midst of his people:

> You brought them in, you planted them
>   on the mountain that is your own—
> The place you made the base of your throne, Lord,
>   the sanctuary, Lord, your hands established.
>   (Exod 15:17)

It certainly cannot be denied that the Song of the Sea is characterized by strong expressions, such as "the Lord is a warrior" (Exod 15:3)—literally, "he is a man of war" (*îš milhamâ*)—and "your right hand, O Lord, shattered the enemy" (Exod 15:6). These images of God are inconsistent with the face of the merciful Father offered by Jesus in the Gospel.

The rabbinic tradition, commenting on this account of the Exodus, shows a certain unease with the Song of the Sea and its excess of punishment and militarism. The *Megîllâ* treatise of the Talmud narrates that God, in his compassion, ordered the angels not to sing the song of victory together with the children of Israel: "After the children of Israel arrived safely on dry land, once again the angels attempted to raise their song of praise and prayer. However, the Almighty once again refused them permission and said to them: 'The work of my hands sinks into the sea, and you want to sing? My compassion includes all living beings. How could I accept your singing in such circumstances?'"[12]

Rabbinic literature, then, reveals a significant ethical sensitivity also towards the law of Moses, attributing to God both justice and compassion. The wisdom of Solomon shows ambivalence, too, stating that "when the wicked perish, there is jubilation" (Prov 11:10), but further on, "Do not rejoice when your enemies fall, / and when they stumble, do not let your heart exult" (Prov 24:17). In the two shores of the Red Sea between which Israel walks on dry land, the rabbinic tradition sees the metaphor of the need to walk in the middle between justice and mercy,

---

12. *Talmud, Megîllâ* 10b; see also *Sanhedhrîn* 39b.

without drowning in war and hatred. Maimonides called this middle path between the shores of the sea "the path of the wise."[13]

We, too, can affirm that in commemorating Israel's Passover by celebrating that of Jesus Christ, we as Christians ought to give within our liturgy a sign that balances justice with mercy, rather than offering a literal reading of Exodus 15's song of victory. It is probably no coincidence that the Easter Vigil is the only place where the Song of the Sea appears in the Roman liturgy and that it is absent among the many Old Testament canticles of the Liturgy of the Hours, even in the Easter season.[14] In the wake of the conciliar reform of the liturgy—which sought a greater fidelity of the rite to the Christian message, to pastoral concerns, and to what Pope Paul VI (referring, in fact, to the Easter Vigil) called "adapting . . . to the contemporary mentality"[15]—the canticle of Exodus 15 might be replaced by other canticles—such as Isaiah 12, for example—or by extracts from historical psalms in which the liberation of Israel is narrated, such as Psalm 105, Psalm 107, or even the great Hallel, Psalm 136. In the same way, the parallel text of Exodus 12:37-42,

13. *Hilchot Deot* 1, 4.

14. Therefore, the note from *The Jerusalem Bible* to Exod 15:1-21 seems incongruous when it calls this passage "the first and most famous of the 'canticles' which the Christian liturgy takes from the [Old Testament]." *The Jerusalem Bible* (Garden City, NY: Doubleday, 1966), 95.

15. "A beginning was made by Pius XII in the restoration of the Easter Vigil and Holy Week services; he thus took the first step toward adapting the Roman Missal to the contemporary mentality." Paul VI, Apostolic Constitution *Missale Romanum* (April 3, 1969), in *Documents on the Liturgy 1963–1979: Conciliar, Papal, and Curial Texts* (Collegeville, MN: Liturgical Press, 1982), 458.

which narrates the departure of Israel from Egypt on "a night of vigil for the LORD" (v. 42), could be offered as an alternative to the reading of the Red Sea passage of Exodus 14.

The prayer concludes this third section of the Liturgy of the Word:

> O God, whose ancient wonders
> remain undimmed in splendor even in our day,
> for what you once bestowed on a single people,
> freeing them from Pharoah's persecution
> by the power of your right hand,
> now you bring about as the salvation of the nations
> through the waters of rebirth,
> grant, we pray, that the whole world
> may become children of Abraham
> and inherit the dignity of Israel's birthright.[16]

Placing baptism at the center, this prayer is an eloquent example of a sacramental interpretation of biblical texts. The event that the passage from the book of Exodus recounts happens today in the baptismal immersion that will take place shortly after the Liturgy of the Word. The link between the waters of the Red Sea and those of the baptismal font is the dominant image, so that the liturgical context becomes the hermeneutic *locus* of the Scriptures. The Italian translation makes the baptismal interpretation all the more explicit by rendering the expression *"per acquam regenerationis"* as "through the water of Baptism."

The prayer then offers a universalist perspective of salvation: from the liberation of "a single people," Israel, to

16. *The Roman Missal*, 366.

"the salvation of the nations," all of humanity. The concluding petition prays that the people of the whole world may become children of Abraham, thus evoking the fulfillment of the promise made by the Lord to Abraham: "All the families of the earth will find blessing in you" (Gen 12:3). The original Latin of this prayer offers an important theological nuance that the Italian text fails to translate: it asks that the people of the whole world "fully become" children of Abraham (*In Abrahae filios . . . totius mundi transeat plenitudo*).[17] The concept of fullness opens up an eschatological dimension of great importance, placing the celebration of the Vigil in the perspective of the eternal Passover now celebrated only in the sacrament.

The second prayer option also expresses, in different words, the same parallelism between the Red Sea and baptismal immersion:

> O God, who by the light of the New Testament
> have unlocked the meaning
> of wonders worked in former times,
> so that the Red Sea prefigures the sacred font
> and the nation delivered from slavery
> foreshadows the Christian people,
> grant, we pray, that all nations,
> obtaining the privilege of Israel by merit of faith,
> may be reborn by partaking of your Spirit.[18]

17. The author points out here that the Italian liturgical translation does not translate the word *plenitudo* from the Latin original; the same is true of the official English translation as well. —Trans.

18. *The Roman Missal*, 366.

It states that God himself illuminates for us, with the light of the New Testament, the meaning of the actions he performed in the first covenant. The Red Sea is the image of the baptismal font, and the people of Israel are the symbol of the Christian people. In summary, in the sacramental interpretation of the biblical texts, baptism fulfills the event narrated in the story of the Exodus.

The prayer that concludes the Liturgy of the Word is of great interest, because it expresses the purpose of prolonged listening to the biblical passages: that of teaching us how to celebrate Easter:

> O God, who by the pages of both Testaments
> instruct and prepare us to celebrate the Paschal
>   Mystery,
> grant that we may comprehend your mercy,
> so that the gifts we receive from you this night
> may confirm our hope of the gifts to come.[19]

19. *The Roman Missal*, 368.

Chapter 3

The Liturgy of Water

The water of life

After the fire, light, and word, we come to the other great principle of life that, in the Easter Vigil liturgy, becomes matter and symbol to celebrate the resurrection of Christ: water. In its simplicity, water is the substance of life down to the most microscopic cells. It is both mother and matrix. Of every living organism, animal or plant, water is a fundamental component. They depend on water: without water there is no life. Indeed, water bears life, to the point of being such a vital force that nothing and no one can stop it, neither obstacles, nor embankments, nor walls. Water covers more than seventy percent of the planet's surface, and the human body itself is made up of two-thirds water, which makes it a primary and precious resource for the earth and for human life. Water is the only natural element that can rightly be identified tout court with life: water is life. It quenches thirst, makes what is withered flourish, regenerates what is desiccated, resurrects what seems dead.

In various religions, water is linked to the origin of the world and of life, and therefore it is an element of salvation, because for humans, as for every living being, access to water is a matter of life or death. But it is also associated with the experience of the universal flood, a natural catastrophe associated, however, with purification in view of a covenant, as we see in the book of Genesis. Due to its connatural property of washing and cleaning, water is associated in various religions with purification from impurity, in the form of immersion in rivers or springs, in ritual baths, or through ablution.

From the "mighty wind sweeping over the waters" (Gen 1:2) on the first page of Genesis to "the spring of life-giving water" (Rev 21:6) in the vision of the Apocalypse, water flows through the Bible from end to end. The Targum interprets the source of life in Psalm 36—"With you is the fountain of life, / and in your light we see light" (v. 10)—as a source of living water: "From you gushes forth living water, in the splendor of your glory we will see light." Quenched with water and illuminated by light, the psalmist recognizes and confesses God's salvation. Through the mouth of the prophet Jeremiah, the Lord describes himself as a source of living water, while the people prefer to dig cracked cisterns for themselves:

> Two evils my people have done:
> they have forsaken me, the source of living waters;
> They have dug themselves cisterns,
> broken cisterns that cannot hold water. (Jer 2:13)

In his vision, Ezekiel sees water flowing out of the new temple in Jerusalem, a sign of God's blessing that returns to dwell among his people after exile (cf. Ezek 47:1-12).

Throughout the Bible, rivers, springs, and wells are the places where the history of salvation happens, where life flows and springs forth.

In the New Testament, it is above all the evangelist John who tells us, in the encounter with the Samaritan woman at Jacob's well, that the messianic gift of Jesus is "living water" (John 4:11) and shows us Jesus, speaking as Wisdom at the temple in Jerusalem, promising: "Let anyone who thirsts come to me and drink. . . . 'Rivers of living water will flow from within him'" (John 7:37-38). Water is the final and intense desire of Jesus on the cross: "I thirst" (John 19:28). In the First Letter of John, there are three elements that testify to God's revelation in Jesus Christ: "There are three that testify, the Spirit, the water, and the blood, and the three are of one accord" (1 John 5:7-8). The testimony of water is baptismal immersion, which for the apostle Paul is "the bath of rebirth / and renewal by the holy Spirit" (Titus 3:5).

In the biblical tradition, then, water is associated with life, purification, rebirth, and salvation, and the liturgy takes up all of these meanings fully. The link between Easter and water is also represented by a tradition in Western peasant culture, practiced in many places until the 1950s: the Easter Vigil was celebrated in those days on the morning of Holy Saturday, and at the sound of the bells ringing out, people went to the streams to wash their eyes, a sign of purification and renewal.

The baptismal Passover

Listening to the word of God in the great biblical passages from the law of Moses, the prophets, and the psalms reaches its climax in the proclamation of the gospel of Christ's resurrection. The reading of the apostle Paul (Rom 6:3-11) serves as a bridge between the Old and the New Testaments and, at the same time, confirms the baptismal interpretation of the biblical texts already offered in the prayers that have followed them. Paul draws a parallel between Jesus' death on the cross and burial, and Christian baptism. As the risen Christ rises from the tomb, so the Christian emerges from the baptismal font as a new creature. Once again, we see the effectiveness of the liturgical context and the full correspondence between the pages of the New Testament and the liturgy of the church. Soon what the apostle proclaims will become reality: those buried with Christ through baptism will be resurrected together with him (cf. Col 2:12). In the Vigil, the celebration of Christ's Passover takes place sacramentally in the baptismal Passover of Christians through baptismal immersion, anointing with holy chrism, and participation in the eucharistic table. In what follows, we will not comment fully on the rites of baptism; we will simply gather some insights from the liturgical context within which they are performed.

The Order of Christian Initiation of Adults calls for the initiation of adults to be celebrated, according to tradition, on the sacred night of the Easter Vigil. Thus baptism finds its vital context in the Easter Vigil, which strongly links baptism to the paschal mystery in its most intense expression. In other words, placing baptism in the Vigil means placing it within the liturgical assembly par excellence: that which celebrates the feast of Easter. Baptism is the sacrament through which one enters the church, and this is why everything in the baptismal liturgy testifies that baptism can only be understood as an act and an event of the church, of which the liturgical assembly is the highest epiphany.

Within the Easter Vigil, the baptismal rites immediately follow the long Liturgy of the Word. Even when it is celebrated outside the Vigil, the Liturgy of the Word always precedes baptism, because without the proclamation of the word of God, the sacrament would be amputated and lose its Christian specificity. After the Liturgy of the Word is the celebration of baptism, which is made up of five elements: the litany of the saints, the blessing of the water, the renunciation of sin and profession of faith, the baptismal immersion, and, finally, the explanatory rites: the dressing in the white garment and the handing over of the lighted candle.

The baptismal liturgy opens with the litany of the saints, with which the assembly invokes its fathers and mothers in faith. Through the singing of the litany of the saints, the liturgy reminds us that what is transmitted to those who will receive baptism is none other than the faith of the fathers of the first covenant, what was received by the apostles and handed down from generation to generation by Christ's faithful witnesses. Entering the church through baptism means being united not only with the present-day body of Christ but also with its past, with the entire history of the holy people of God and the entire history of the church, with both its shadows and its lights. Placed within the Easter Vigil, it would be extremely significant if the litany invoked the saints of the Old Testament, especially Abraham and Moses, the great biblical figures evoked in the pages of Scripture just heard. Receiving new life in Christ through baptism means entering fully into the whole history of salvation lived by men and women of faith of the old and new covenant, those known and unknown, who, as the Roman Canon states, "have gone before us with the sign of faith / and rest in the sleep of peace."[1] Ultimately, the singing of the litany of the saints is the highest liturgical expression of the "communion of saints" of heaven and earth.

After the litany of the saints, what the ritual calls the Blessing of Baptismal Water takes place. In reality, there is no blessing of the water in the text, which is why the French ritual identifies it more accurately: a blessing of God and invocation of God upon the water. After all, water, as we have seen, is the most blessed element that exists in nature. The authentic meaning of the biblical blessing (the *berakhâ*) is that God is blessed for his gift of water, just as in the *berakhôth* of the presentation of the gifts, the Lord is blessed for the bread and wine.

The baptismal liturgy takes up the biblical ambivalence of water as both the principle of life and a force of death. Every creation (Genesis 1), every new creation (flood), every passage from a place of death (Egypt) to the land of life (crossing the Red Sea) is reread according to the great passage (Passover) made by Christ for the whole humanity and applied symbolically to baptism. For this reason, in the mystagogical catecheses of the fathers of the church, the creation, the flood, and the crossing of the Red Sea are the main typological figures of baptism. These figures are reflected in the Blessing of Baptismal Water, which is a great anamnesis of the role of water in the history of salvation. The benchmarks of this history are out-

---

1. *The Roman Missal*, 642.

lined as a true and proper *preparatio acquae* ("O God, who . . . have prepared water, your creation, / to show forth the grace of Baptism . . ." the presider prays at the beginning of the blessing upon the water) for the baptismal immersion of Christ in the waters of the Jordan and the Christian in the baptismal font. This blessing upon the water is a sort of doxological repetition of what has just been heard in the Liturgy of the Word. Here are the most significant passages:

> O God, whose Spirit
> in the first moments of the world's creation
> hovered over the waters,
> so that the very substance of water
> would even then take to itself the power to sanctify;
>
> O God, who by the outpouring of the flood
> foreshadowed regeneration,
> so that from the mystery of one and the same
>   element of water
> would come an end to vice and a beginning of virtue;
>
> O God, who caused the children of Abraham
> to pass dry-shod through the Red Sea,
> so that the chosen people,
> set free from slavery to Pharaoh,
> would prefigure the people of the baptized;
>
> O God, whose Son,
> baptized by John in the waters of the Jordan,
> was anointed with the Holy Spirit,
> and, as he hung upon the Cross,
> gave forth water from his side along with blood . . .
> look now, we pray, upon the face of your Church
> and graciously unseal for her the fountain of Baptism.

> May this water receive by the Holy Spirit
> the grace of your Only Begotten Son,
> so that human nature, created in your image
> and washed clean through the Sacrament of Baptism
> from all the squalor of the life of old,
> may be found worthy to rise to the life of newborn
>   children
> through water and the Holy Spirit.
>
> May the power of the Holy Spirit,
> O Lord, we pray,
> come down through your Son
> into the fullness of this font,
> so that all who have been buried with Christ
> by Baptism into death
> may rise again to life with him.[2]

This great anamnesis of water, culminating in the epiclesis, the invocation of the Spirit upon the water, bears witness to the fact that the baptismal symbolism is inseparable from the Holy Spirit. Here, the liturgy purely echoes the New Testament, which attests to the necessary birth "of water and Spirit" (John 3:5), as Jesus says to Nicodemus, and which distinguishes John the Baptist's water baptism from the baptism in the Spirit given by Jesus. To those who allow themselves to be immersed by him in the Jordan, the Baptist announces the baptism in the Holy Spirit: "I am baptizing you with water, for repentance, but the one who is coming after me . . . will baptize you with the holy Spirit and fire" (Matt 3:11).

The liturgical and theological importance of the invocation of the Spirit on the baptismal water is therefore

---

2. *The Roman Missal*, 377–78.

enormous. This epiclesis is already attested in the third century, among others by Tertullian. St. Ambrose of Milan comments upon it as follows: "The action [of baptism] belongs to the water, its effect to the Holy Spirit. The water does not heal unless the Spirit descends and consecrates the water."[3]

Understanding this great symbolic richness of water and of immersion in it, we can see better how baptism administered by affusion, as happens almost exclusively today in the Catholic Church, considerably reduces the value and meaning of the symbolism and the materiality of water, especially at the Easter Vigil. It is not reduced philosophically, as was the case in scholastic sacramental theology, but in the value of the material elements of which the liturgy makes use: water, oil, bread, wine, and again wax, fire, ashes, and so on. Let us ask ourselves why we Westerners are afraid of matter—of "blessed matter," as Teilhard de Chardin called it. Why this embarrassment and this incapacity before the natural elements that the liturgy uses? We should not focus exclusively on those who receive the sacraments, on their preparation and their interior dispositions, to the detriment of the value of the liturgical symbol itself. The liturgy is not a question of "ideas," but of "body," of corporality. The weaker and more poorly enacted the signs and the liturgical gestures are, the more their bodily perception is devalued and compromised. A badly done liturgical symbol is equivalent to a badly done translation of the Scriptures or to badly done preaching.

---

3. Ambrose of Milan, *De Sacramentis* I, 15, in Edward Yarnold, ed., *The Awe-Inspiring Rites of Initiation: The Origins of the RCIA*, 2nd ed. (Collegeville, MN: Liturgical Press, 1994), 100–149, at 105.

If baptism is not administered at the Easter Vigil, the presider invokes the blessing upon the water for the sprinkling of the assembly, as a reminder of their own baptisms. This text of the blessing highlights other aspects of the mystery of water than the previous one. The natural value of water itself is emphasized—"you created water to make the fields fruitful / and to refresh and cleanse our bodies"—and it is recognized as a sign of God's mercy and interpreted as a sign of the new covenant announced by the prophets.

> Lord our God,
> in your mercy be present to your people
> who keep vigil on this most sacred night,
> and, for us who recall the wondrous work of our creation
> and the still greater work of our redemption,
> graciously bless this water.
> For you created water to make the fields fruitful
> and to refresh and cleanse our bodies.
> You also made water the instrument of your mercy:
> for through water you freed your people from slavery
> and quenched their thirst in the desert;
> through water the Prophets proclaimed the new covenant
> you were to enter upon with the human race;
> and last of all,
> through water, which Christ made holy in the Jordan,
> you have renewed our corrupted nature
> in the bath of regeneration.
> Therefore, may this water be for us
> a memorial of the Baptism we have received,
> and grant that we may share
> in the gladness of our brothers and sisters,
> who at Easter have received their Baptism.[4]

4. *The Roman Missal*, 381.

After the blessing and the epiclesis upon the water, the renunciation (*abrenuntiatio*) and the profession of faith (*professio fidei*)—two sides of the same coin—take place. In the context of initiation, this phase marks the transition from a negative condition to a positive one. With the triple renunciation of Satan, the catechumens declare that they abandon all that is contrary to the Gospel. In the Vigil, if baptism has not been celebrated, after the blessing upon the water, the faithful present, holding the lighted candles in their hands, renew their baptismal promises. The words of the first and most ancient formula are repeated nearly verbatim today:

> Priest: Do you renounce Satan?
> All: I do.
> Priest: And all his works?
> All: I do.
> Priest: And all his empty show?
> All: I do.

Following the threefold renunciation of Satan comes the threefold profession of faith, in which the church has always recognized an essential moment of baptism. It is a trinitarian profession of faith made up of three questions and a triple response of "I do":

> Priest: Do you believe in God,
>   the Father almighty,
>   Creator of heaven and earth?
> All: I do.
> Priest: Do you believe in Jesus Christ, his only
>   Son . . .?

All: I do.
Priest: Do you believe in the Holy Spirit,
          the holy Catholic Church,
          the communion of saints . . . ?
All: I do.[5]

In the Order of Baptism of Children, the presider concludes with the beautiful formula, "This is our faith. This
is the faith of the Church. We are proud to profess it in
Christ Jesus our Lord," to which the assembly responds,
"Amen."[6]

I would like to emphasize just one aspect of this renunciation of Satan and profession of faith: the symbolic importance of the dialogical structure of this rite, made up
of three questions and three answers. And it is significant
that the renewal of baptismal promises is also done in a
dialogical form. From this simple element we can see that
the liturgy makes clear that no one can declare himself a
Christian: only the church can do so. And the church does
not ask the baptized what are his opinions about God but
whether he is willing to express the trinitarian faith that
the church received from the apostles. This explains why,
to become a Christian, there is a need for a sacrament: the
sacrament of baptism (which is also called, not by chance,
"the sacrament of faith") can never be reduced to one's
capacity for interior conversion and personal decision.

The personal response "I do" to the question "Do you
believe?" also means the personal assumption of the Chris-

---

5. *The Roman Missal*, 382–83.

6. *The Order of Baptism of Children* (Collegeville, MN: Liturgical Press,
2017), 31.

tian faith, which from that moment no longer belongs only to the church but also to the baptized.

In the Easter Vigil, the liturgy of water concludes with the sprinkling of the assembly and therefore with a physical and direct contact between the water and the bodies of those present. The sprinkling is accompanied by the antiphon taken from the prophecy of Ezekiel 47 and his vision of the water flowing from the temple, which opens the entire assembly to an eschatological perspective of great significance and undoubted effectiveness. Once again, the relationship between water and salvation that runs through the entire Vigil is highlighted:

> I saw water flowing from the Temple,
> from its right-hand side, alleluia;
> and all to whom this water came were saved
> and shall say: Alleluia, alleluia.[7]

7. *The Roman Missal*, 384.

CHAPTER 4

The Liturgy of the Table

THE EUCHARIST, PASCHAL SACRAMENT

The Savior . . . promised [the disciples] that they should no longer eat the flesh of a lamb, but His own, saying, 'Take, eat and drink; this is My body, and My blood.' When we are then nourished by these things, we shall also, my beloved, properly keep the feast of the Passover," wrote Athanasius of Alexandria.[1] The Eucharist is the paschal sacrament because Jesus performed the gesture of breaking bread for his disciples in the context of the Jewish feast of Passover and above all in reference to his own Passover, when "his hour had come to pass from this world to the Father" (John 13:1). On the eve of his passion, Jesus performed actions that transformed a journey of suffering and death into conviviality and gift. On the night he was betrayed, he sat at table with his disciples and broke bread; on the day he rose again, he sat at table and broke bread with them again. The breaking of bread

---

1. Athanasius of Alexandria, Letter IV, in *The Festal Epistles of S. Athanasius* (London: F. and J. Rivington, 1854), 34–35.

and the Lord's table are inseparable. Gathering at the table is one with the breaking of bread, because breaking bread only makes sense in a convivial context, as the gospel stories of the Last Supper and Emmaus attest. From Easter day, gathering as a community of faith around the "table of the Lord" (1 Cor 10:21) to break bread and drink from the one cup means acknowledging that Christ is risen and alive in the midst of his community. In obedience to the mandate to "do this in memory of me" (Luke 22:19), the Eucharist has been the Christian Passover rite since the New Testament.

By freeing the Eucharist from being reduced to only "sacrifice of the cross," the Second Vatican Council restored it to its original nature as a paschal mystery, placing it in relation not only to the Lord's death but also to his resurrection and the Parousia. The council confessed the Eucharist to be "a memorial of his death and resurrection . . . a paschal banquet,"[2] and that in it "is contained the entire spiritual wealth of the church, namely Christ himself our Pasch and our living bread, who gives life to people through his flesh—that flesh which is given life and gives life by the holy Spirit."[3] The liturgy of the Octave of Easter itself refers to the Eucharist as "this paschal Sacrament."[4] Celebrating the Eucharist is celebrating the

2. Second Vatican Council, Constitution on the Sacred Liturgy *Sacrosanctum Concilium* (December 4, 1963), n. 47, in Austin Flannery, OP, ed., *Vatican Council II: Constitutions, Decrees, Declarations; The Basic Sixteen Documents* (Collegeville, MN: Liturgical Press, 2014), 135.

3. Second Vatican Council, Decree on the Ministry and Life of Priests *Presbyterorum Ordinis* (December 7, 1965), n. 5, in Flannery, *Vatican Council II*, 325.

4. *The Roman Missal*, "Prayer after Communion," 389.

Christian Passover, it is celebrating Easter, as the assembly acclaims by turning to Christ himself after hearing his words over the bread and the chalice: "We proclaim your Death, O Lord, / and profess your Resurrection / until you come again."[5] The liturgy is therefore the greatest witness of the great and uninterrupted tradition of faith of the church, which even a medieval author like Paschasius Radbertus (785–865) has always recognized: "The flesh of Christ has become the Eucharist thanks to the resurrection."[6]

The starting point and, at the same time, the point of arrival of every possible reflection on the Eucharist is the mystery of which it is a sacrament: the mystery of the paschal Christ. For this reason, the Eucharist celebrated in the context of the Easter Vigil finds itself most at home and in the fullest expression of its meaning, because the liturgical assembly that watches in the night to celebrate the Passover of its Lord is the highest and most eloquent epiphany of the church, body of the paschal Christ. For this reason, the Vigil is the natural place where one becomes a Christian and fully enters the church by becoming new creatures in the baptismal immersion, in the anointing with the holy chrism, and in the participation in the eucharistic table. The people who make up the believing community welcome new sisters and brothers with whom they form the living body of the Risen One. It is not a perfect and flawless body; it is wounded, fragile, marked by sin, divisions, and even scandals. And yet it is a living body even when it seems moribund, as the church

5. *The Roman Missal*, 640.
6. Paschasius Radbertus, *De corpore et sanguine Domini* V, 24.

in the West does in our day. Yet it is the paschal body of Christ, and in it lives the life of the Risen One, a life incessantly revitalized by the Holy Spirit, who is "Lord and giver of life," as we profess in the Creed.

By forgetting for almost a millennium the link between the Eucharist and the resurrection of Christ, Western Christianity weakened the understanding that the Christians of the first centuries had of the Eucharist as "the medicine of immortality and the antidote that wards off death," as Ignatius of Antioch wrote to the Christians of Ephesus.[7] Faced with the heretics who denied the reality of the body, Irenaeus of Lyons affirmed: "Our bodies that receive the Eucharist are no longer corruptible."[8] What is at stake in this link between the Eucharist and the resurrection is immortality, understood as the seed of the resurrection which is the fruit of death to oneself: "Unless a grain of wheat falls to the ground and dies, it remains just a grain of wheat; but if it dies, it produces much fruit. Whoever loves his life loses it, and whoever hates his life in this world will preserve it for eternal life" (John 12:24-25). These are the most eucharistic verses of the New Testament because they illustrate the paschal logic of the Eucharist.

"Whoever eats this bread will live forever" (John 6:58). The Eucharist does not prevent the believer from dying but saves her from death, because the Eucharist allows one to live in death. The opposite of life is not death but birth; the purpose of the Gospel, in fact, is not to prevent us from

7. Ignatius of Antioch, *Letter to the Ephesians*, 20.
8. Irenaeus of Lyons, *Against Heresies*, 18, 5.

dying but to make us reborn to true life. The Eucharist is a paschal sacrament because, like the Passover of Christ, it does not eliminate bodily death but takes possession of it and gives it a new birth, makes of it a communion. This is the paschal name of the Eucharist: communion. The body of the Risen One is a body of communion, just as broken bread is a bread of communion.

THE TABLE OF THE RISEN ONE

After experiencing the fundamental symbols of life in all its forms—fire, light, word, water—and having reached the eucharistic liturgy, the Easter Vigil brings the faithful to the experience of the summit and synthesis of the symbols of life: the table. At the eucharistic table, we find the symbols of life that marked the celebration of the Passover night: light and fire in the flame of candles, water, the word spoken and heard, and, added to these, the gifts of bread and wine.

Eating together at the same table is the reality and simultaneously the metaphor of the essence and purpose of human life: being in one another's presence, looking one another in the face, having the word in common while sharing bread, food, and wine of joy. The table is a place of hospitality, space and time for understanding and exchange, somehow feeding on each other like food that is eaten together, nourishing the spirit as well as the body. It is an experience of recognition and sometimes even of reconciliation, so that the table is the place where simple existence together becomes communion. Understood and lived in all its value, the table is the most eloquent analogy of the church, mystery of communion. As I have already written at length, the Christian community is a table community.[9]

While the Eucharist always and in every circumstance tells the truth of itself and of its being "mystery of faith," it assumes a unique and unrepeatable connotation when it is celebrated at the Easter Vigil and throughout the fifty days of the Easter season. The eucharistic table of the Vigil is the table of the Risen One, a memorial of the meals at Emmaus, in the upper room in Jerusalem, and on Lake Tiberias. It is very significant that the table and eating together play such an important role in the gospel accounts of the disciples' encounters with the Risen One. In these common meals of Jesus with the disciples, the church was born as communion with the paschal Christ. The church was born there because each of the tables of the Risen One is an experience of joy after the days of pain, an encounter after the dispersion, recognition after the experience of disfiguring suffering. The table of the Risen One is also a place of forgiveness of infidelity, reconciliation and communion after denial, and following that replaces flight, abandonment, and dispersion. It is the table at which the wedding supper of the slaughtered Lamb is celebrated, where mortal wounds are not hidden but transfigured by love. At the table of the risen Christ, the deepest truth of Christianity is revealed.

The fire that warms, the light that illuminates, the water and the table of bread that satisfies and wine that gladdens the heart—Easter is a feast, and feasting means the con-

9. See Goffredo Boselli, "Il Vangelo della tavola," in Boselli, *Sorgente di vita: Liturgia e ricerca spirituale* (Cinisello Balsamo: San Paolo, 2017), 29–60.

viviality of the table, of communion, and of sharing. Christianity was born at the Passover table where Jesus is recognized as Lord, and at the Easter Vigil the community of Jesus' disciples gathers around his table above all to confess him as "the one who lives" (Rev 1:18) in a feast that is encounter, shared meal, fraternity, welcome, and belonging. The eucharistic community is a table community that celebrates Christ, the Lamb of the eternal Passover.

CHAPTER 5

The Day the Lord Has Made

"I have risen"

Resurrexi, et adhuc tecum sum, alleluia.

After the many rites, the innumerable words, the confessions of faith, the alleluias, the exultant acclamations, and the songs of joy of the Easter Vigil, at the dawn of the day without sunset the church does not speak but allows Christ to speak, Christ who addresses the Father, saying in the entrance antiphon of Easter morning, "I have risen, and I am with you still. . . ."[1] The translation of the Italian Missal makes clear the addressee of Christ's words: "I have risen, Father, and I am always with you." The voice that resonates at the rising of the Easter sun is not the voice of the church but of the Risen One.

Gregorian scholars observe that the antiphon *Resurrexi* is a restrained chant that, instead of indulging in a cry of joy, invites us to a subdued song. The composer Gianmartino Maria Durighello observes: "After so much waiting, we would have expected to sing Alleluia with overflowing

---

1. *The Roman Missal*, 387.

93

joy, and instead the chant seems to want to lead us to silence. We would have expected to sing a song capable of rising high, to paint the resurrection even visually, and instead we find the total absence of movement and momentum, forced into a melodic environment of a few notes."[2]

It is not the *jubilus* of the gradual *Haec dies* of the same Mass, nor is it a triumphal song in the Doric mode, like the sequence *Victimae paschali laudes*, which narrates the victorious outcome of a monumental duel between life and death and concludes with the bold and almost prideful certainty: *Scimus Christum surrexisse a mortuis vere*. No, there is none of this in the entrance antiphon, which is instead in the fourth tone, which, in the Gregorian *octoechos*, is generally the tone of mourning and unhappiness. Here, however, it expresses that intimacy and confidence that befit a dialogue between the son who "was dead and came back to life" and finds his father again—Jesus, the prodigal of the Father, as Henri Denis would say.[3]

The most important introit of the Gregorian repertoire, as this antiphon is said to be, is the only instance in which the liturgy chooses not to speak of the Risen One in the third person, but rather to let the Risen One speak in the first person. Not *Resurrexit*, "he has risen," but *Resurrexi*, "I have risen." If in the Easter Vigil the church repeated in many different forms and ways what the resurrection is *for it*, in the incipit of Easter day it allows the Risen One to say what his resurrection is *for him*. The discreet

2. Gianmartino Maria Durighello, "Resurrexi," Paulus 2.0, https://letterepaoline.net/2009/04/11/.

3. See Henri Denis, *Gesù il prodigo del Padre* (Assisi: Cittadella, 2003).

and restrained Gregorian melody seems to want to musically convey the voice of the Risen One himself, which is the voice of a man who has suffered, the voice of an innocent victim filled with the memory of the days of the passion. Jesus could narrate his resurrection in many different ways; here he chooses only one. Christ announces his resurrection not as a victory over death, not as a triumph over hell, not as the defeat of enemies or as the conquest of eternal life, but in a dialogue from Son to Father he confesses that to rise again means to be with the Father again.[4] Returning to life for the Son meant returning to being with the Father, to live again and forever the same life as the Father, thus reuniting with his own origin:

> In the beginning was the Word,
> > and the Word was with God,
> > and the Word was God. (John 1:1)

Here is the text of the introit in its entirety, followed by the translation of the English edition of the Roman Missal:

> *Resurrexi, et adhuc tecum sum, alleluia.*
> *Posuisti super me manum tuam, alleluia.*
> *Mirabilis facta est scientia tua, alleluia, alleluia.*
> *Domine probasti me, et cognovisti me:*
> *tu cognovisti sessionem meam, et resurrectionem meam.*

4. We should not fail to notice the massive distance between the belligerent tone of the Song of the Sea and the peaceful tone of the Son addressing the Father.

I have risen, and I am with you still, alleluia.
You have laid your hand upon me, alleluia.
Too wonderful for me, this knowledge, alleluia, alleluia.[5]

The text of the entrance antiphon is taken from an ancient Latin version of Psalm 139. The Latin text and that of the Greek version of the LXX of the psalter correspond perfectly in v. 18: "I have risen, and I am with you still." For the Eastern and Western Christian tradition, it is one of the most immediately christological passages of the Old Testament, in which the church has recognized a clear prophecy of the resurrection of Jesus. Easter reveals the importance that the church attributes to it. The whole of Psalm 139 is a dialogue of love between the believer and God: "LORD, you have probed me, you know me" (v. 1). It is a confession of the knowledge of God in the sense of being known by him from the womb, of his constant presence by which he does not abandon us even in hell, in the experience of darkness or even in sleep: "When I awake, I am still with you" (v. 18, NIV). If, as is often the case in biblical thought, sleep is a metaphor for death, the person praying confesses his being with God upon awakening in the resurrection. The interpretation of this verse given by the Greek version of the psalter and by extension the Latin one, as we have seen, is rooted in the Hebrew text.

At his 2007 Easter Vigil Mass, Pope Benedict XVI centered his homily on the text of the antiphon *Resurrexi*, offering a valuable mystagogy. Benedict interprets the spiritual journey of the person praying in Psalm 139 as the paschal experience of Christ and also considers the

5. *The Roman Missal*, 387.

dialogue of the antiphon as words that the Risen One addresses to the church:

> The vision of the Psalm thus became reality. In the impenetrable gloom of death Christ came like light—the night became as bright as day and the darkness became as light. And so the Church can rightly consider these words of thanksgiving and trust as words spoken by the Risen Lord to his Father: "Yes, I have journeyed to the uttermost depths of the earth, to the abyss of death, and brought them light; now I have risen and I am upheld for ever by your hands." But these words of the Risen Christ to the Father have also become words which the Lord speaks to us: "I arose and now I am still with you," he says to each of us. My hand upholds you. Wherever you may fall, you will always fall into my hands. I am present even at the door of death. Where no one can accompany you further, and where you can bring nothing, even there I am waiting for you, and for you I will change darkness into light.[6]

"I LIVE AND YOU WILL LIVE"

It is, therefore, thanks to the liturgy that the Risen One bears witness to his own resurrection. After all, never in the New Testament does Jesus refer to himself as "the Risen One." In the so-called farewell speeches of the Fourth Gospel, which is a rereading of the life of Jesus in

6. Pope Benedict XVI, Easter Vigil homily, April 7, 2007, https:// www.vatican.va/content/benedict-xvi/en/homilies/2007/documents /hf_ben-xvi_hom_20070407_veglia-pasquale.html.

the light of Easter, he declares, "I live and you will live" (John 14:19), a promise of life that is the Easter proclamation of the living Lord. Only the Living One can promise life. The word of the Risen One in another Johannine text, the book of Revelation, finds an echo here: "Do not be afraid. I am the first and the last, the one who lives. Once I was dead, but now I am alive forever and ever" (Rev 1:17-18). "Do not be afraid. I am . . . the one who lives"—that is to say, "Don't be afraid. I live and that means you will live too—do not doubt it!" The Living One is not only the one who once gave his life for us but the one who in this moment gives us life, in the sense that he promises life, makes us believe in life, makes us hope for life—not only life after death, but life before death, the one we live now. Life during life!

The Johannine community held the conviction that believing that Christ has conquered death means nothing other than believing that the life lived by Jesus is still today a promise of life for us. To confess that Christ has risen is to believe that his life was not buried with him in the tomb but went through death without death overcoming it. At the dawn of Christianity as well as today, the most credible testimonies of the resurrection of Jesus are men and women who believe in the life of Jesus Christ, desire and seek to live his own life, which is the only and true object of the Christian faith. Let us acknowledge it: What else do we Christians have that is truly credible in the eyes of the world if not the life of Jesus Christ?

Then emerges the meaning of the invitation that the Lord addresses to his disciples: "If you love me, you will keep my commandments" (John 14:15). When he speaks of "my commandments," we needn't think only of those commands that Jesus gave, above all the new commandment of love; in "my commandments," why not also see those commandments that Christ obeyed? He calls them "mine" perhaps because they are those inner commandments that he observed and to which he submitted.

The inner commandment that guided the existence of Jesus was to obey life, to consent radically to life, responding to the desire for life of the most varied people who came to him to ask for healing, help, a word, a recognition. Jesus fought a battle for life because he revived others, giving them confidence in themselves and in life. It was a battle for life against every principle of death, be it disease, evil, violence, exclusion, condemnation, or religious legalism.

We will never reach the incandescent core of the paschal mystery and of the Gospel as a whole if we do not come to understand that for Jesus Christ, believing in God is an act of faith in life. It is an expression of that radical trust in life which can and must dwell in the heart of every human being. For this reason, faith in life is the core of the Easter message.

This is the fundamental reason that the Lord has a touching word for us: "I will not leave you orphans; I will come to you" (John 14:18). The orphan hasn't known his father and mother and therefore doesn't know the life that generated him. The orphan does not know to which life he owes life. The Lord has not left us orphans, because we know well the life that has generated us as believers, the life that makes us live. It is the life of the Son, which is in itself the life of the Father and of the Holy Spirit, the Paraclete.

"Whoever has my commandments and observes them is the one who loves me" (John 14:21). In other words: "If you, too, accept the inner commandment that I have obeyed, that of consenting to life and responding to the desire for life that dwells in every heart, then you love me." The Living One today says: "If you love me, live." "If you love me, give life." "If you proclaim me alive, bring life to others." This is Christianity: an art of living and bringing life to others. To give life and not take it away.

This means making sure that our lives as believers, lived together with others, in whatever form they take—in marriage, in family, in community, in the church, in society—are lives that do good to others and not harm. Let them be lives lived together that make us grow in goodness and not that make us mean to each other. Let them be lives lived together that can heal us in spirit and even in body and not lives that make us and others sick. Let them be lives lived together that improve each other and not make us worse. The life of Jesus Christ brought and generated life, and still today it continues to be for many people a principle of life, a reason for living, a hope for life. That is why his name is the Living One.

"I live and you will live." Listening to the Risen Lord's promise of life today means, then, recognizing that the only measure of our Easter faith is our ability to transmit life and to help others live.

The life that we offer to those who live with us is and will always be the proof of our faith in the risen and living Lord.

Subject Index

Scripture Index